MW00999132

1500

HAMILTON BEACH

AIR FRYER OVEN

COOKBOOK

1500 DAYS AFFORDABLE, HEALTHY RECIPES THAT EVERYONE CAN COOK!

KEVIN WRIGHT

Copyright © 2021 by Kevin Wright- All rights reserved.

The content contained within this book may not be reproduced, duplicated, or transmitted without direct written permission from the author or the publisher. Under no circumstances will any blame or legal responsibility be held against the publisher, or author, for any damages, reparation, or monetary loss due to the information contained within this book, either directly or indirectly.

Legal Notice: This book is copyright protected. It is only for personal use. You cannot amend, distribute sell, use, quote or paraphrase any part, or the content within this book, without the consent of the author or publisher.

Disclaimer Notice: Please note the information contained within this document is for educational and entertainment purposes only. All effort has been executed to present accurate, up to date, reliable, complete information. No warranties of any kind are declared or implied. Readers acknowledge that the author is not engaged in the rendering of legal, financial, medical, or professional advice. The content within this book has been derived from various sources. Please consult a licensed professional before attempting any techniques outlined in this book. By reading this document, the reader agrees that under no circumstances is the author responsible for any losses, direct or indirect, that are incurred as a result of the use of the information contained within this document, including, but not limited to, errors, omissions, or inaccuracies.

CONTENTS

INTRODUCTION

What is and How the Hamilton Beach Air Fryer Oven Works

Although standalone air frying appliances have become increasingly popular, the inconvenience of purchasing yet another countertop appliance that takes up extra room isn't always ideal. Fortunately, today's kitchen ranges come in a wide array of styles and configurations to allow for much more than simply baking cookies or casseroles. Many brands of gas and electric ranges now include air fryers that are built right into the oven.

You can cook up incredible feasts on a standard slide-in range, but what if you're looking for something more? Air fryer ranges offer a delicious-tasting alternative to preparing deep-fried foods. Unlike traditional deep fryers that use hot oil, air frying uses specialized convection fans to circulate hot air at high speeds when cooking your favorite foods. It cooks food faster while ensuring even browning on all sides. Best of all, it requires little to no oil compared to traditional deep fryers.

Air fryer ranges let you effortlessly change your oven's settings from conventional baking or heating to air frying. This is especially beneficial for frying up your favorite foods in less time. Both standalone and air fry range ovens work best with specialized cookware and bakeware like air fry trays, baking sheets or baskets that make the cooking process easy. Many air fryer ranges come with the cookware you'll need to begin making amazing meals right away!

Air fryer ovens circulate heat at super-fast rates to deliver faster cooking results. As stated before, they use convection fans to produce hot air and quickly distribute it evenly throughout the appliance. The main advantage of an air fryer oven over a convection oven is that it's better suited for creating that crispy fried taste much more successfully, especially since you use a specific type of basket or tray to help evenly circulate the heat around the food. For example, foods like chicken wings and French fries retain their natural texture and flavor in an air fryer range since the appliance is made to simulate a deep-fried cooking technique.

Benefits You'll Gain from Your Hamilton Beach Air Fryer Oven

1. Drying food

As we all know, food such as melons and biscuits can become damp after a period at home, which affects the taste and seriously affects the storage time of the food, and the electric home oven can re-dry these wet food to the state we just bought. Delicious and healthy.

2. Snacking

Everyone loves food, especially children, who are particularly sensitive to snacking. If you have an electric oven at home, your child can bake bread and biscuits in it and deliciously enjoy the snacks.

3. You can also eat roast meat at home

With the right seasoning, you can grill at home. It's comfortable and clean to eat whatever you want.

4. Ferment dough and make chocolate treats

Put the dough that needs fermenting into an electric oven and set the temperature to the lowest possible setting to get it ready as quickly as possible. The same goes for chocolate, which can be melted and used in any way you like.

5. No oil, very healthy

For example, if you grill meat, you don't need to put oil in it, and during the grilling process, some of the meat's fat will be removed, so it's much healthier than frying or cooking in a pan.

6. Neat and clean

No more frying, no more frying, no more fumes, and no more clean kitchen.

7. Lazy people

When baking food, lay a layer of tinfoil on the baking tray and throw away the tinfoil when you're done, eliminating the need to brush the pan and wash the tray.

8. Keeping food warm

If you have an oven, you can keep the food warm in the oven. You can leave the stove on and use the preheating of the oven to keep the food warm.

Tips for Using Your Hamilton Beach Air Fryer Oven

1. Remove all packing materials and stickers from the inside and outside of the appliance. Be sure that all accessories are included before throwing away any packaging. Remove wrapping from drip tray inside the oven.

2. Gently wipe the exterior of the oven with a clean, damp cloth and dry thoroughly.

3. Use a mild liquid soap and a damp cloth or sponge to wipe the interior walls. Note: Do not use abrasive cleaners, like steel wool pads, as they may damage the finish.

4. Hand wash the broil/baking pan, wire rack, air fryer basket and removable crumb/drip tray. All these accessories are top-rack dishwasher safe.

5. Place the appliance on a flat, heat-resistant surface.

6. Position the appliance at least 2-4" away from the wall or any objects on the countertop.

7. Do not use on heat-sensitive surfaces.

8. Always insert crumb/drip tray when operating appliance.

9. Metal, ovenproof glass or ceramic bakeware without glass lids can be used in the appliance. Be sure that the top of the container is at least 1 ½" away from the upper heating elements on the top interior.

Tips And Tricks on How to Clean Air Fryer Oven

Air fryer Ovens are much easier to clean than deep fryers that use lots of grease or oil. The cooking basket is closed to prevent spattering and any oil that is used goes into the oil pan to be discarded when dinner is over. With these units, air is the new oil! These cook up fish, chicken, and meat to crispy tender brown using a light batter, and are able to cook vegetables and fruit as well. Most of today's air fryers have some parts that go into the dishwasher. But if not, try these methods. Don't use knives, forks, or metal utensils to remove dried caked food from your air fryer. Most air fryers are coated inside with a non-stick product that's easy to ruin. Never use an abrasive cleaner.

Step 1. Wait until the air fryer cools to the touch and unplug it from the wall and the cooker, unless it is hard wired to the unit. Be sure all the old food is out of the interior pot. Never submerge the pot with plug electronics into water; it will be ruined forever.

Step 2. Cleaning the air fryer is uncomplicated. Wash the cooking basket, tray, and pan in dish-washing detergent in hot water. Most of the newer fryer component parts can go into the dishwasher, but not the housing with the electrical port. Wipe down the housing inside and out with dish-washing detergent, rinse, and towel dry.
Some air fryers have magnetic cord attachments to the bottom and some cords plug into the unit.

Step 3. If you have crusty hard food stuck to your air fryer, make a paste of baking soda and water and scrub gently with a sponge or cloth, rinse, and towel dry. You can use this paste gently on the heating element with an old soft toothbrush at the bottom of your air fryer.

Step 4. Let all parts and the air fryer air dry for a few hours too before putting it away.
Tip: Clean the air fryer after each time it's used; don't wait until it's a hard stuck-on mess before cleaning.

Note: The ceramic, stoneware, and lid will not endure abrupt changes in temperature. Therefore, do not fill a hot pot with cold water; it can crack. Ceramic and stoneware are porous materials and when submerged in water over the top, water can enter the material. I did that to one of my baking dishes and it looks horrible now. The bowl can be filled with water and sit but not submerged in water.

BREAKFAST

Orange-glazed Pears

Servings: 4
Cooking Time: 19 Minutes

Ingredients:

- 2 ripe pears
- 1 tablespoon lemon juice
- 1 tablespoon margarine
- Pinch of salt
- Glaze:
- 2 tablespoons sugar
- 3 tablespoons orange juice

Directions:

1. Prepare the pears: peel, cut in half, remove the seeds and fibrous centers with a teaspoon, quarter and brush the pear pieces with the lemon juice, and set aside.
2. Combine the glaze ingredients in an oiled or nonstick 8½ × 8½ × 2-inch square baking (cake) pan.
3. BROIL for 4 minutes, or until the margarine is melted. Remove from the oven, stir to blend, add the pear quarters, and spoon the glaze mixture over the pears to coat well.
4. BROIL for 15 minutes, or until the glaze has thickened and the pears are tender and golden in color. Serve warm or chilled.

Broiled Grapefruit With Cinnamon Brown Sugar

Servings: 4
Cooking Time: 7 Minutes

Ingredients:

- 2 large grapefruit, halved
- 1/4 cup packed light brown sugar
- 1/4 teaspoon ground cinnamon
- 1 tablespoon butter, softened
- 1/4 cup vanilla yogurt
- 2 tablespoons granola

Directions:

1. Preheat the toaster oven to 400°F. Place rack in upper position.
2. Remove all seeds from grapefruit and section with a paring knife. Cut a small slice from the bottom of each grapefruit half to prevent them from rocking. Place grapefruit halves on toaster oven baking pan.
3. In small bowl, mix brown sugar and cinnamon. Sprinkle evenly over top of grapefruit halves. Dot with butter.
4. Broil for 6 to 7 minutes or until brown sugar and butter is bubbly. Top each half with 1 tablespoon yogurt and 1/2 tablespoon granola.

Cheddar Cheese Biscuits

Servings: 8
Cooking Time: 22 Minutes

Ingredients:

- 2⅓ cups self-rising flour
- 2 tablespoons sugar
- ½ cup butter (1 stick), frozen for 15 minutes
- ½ cup grated Cheddar cheese, plus more to melt on top
- 1⅓ cups buttermilk
- 1 cup all-purpose flour, for shaping
- 1 tablespoon butter, melted

Directions:

1. Line a buttered 7-inch metal cake pan with parchment paper or a silicone liner.

2. Combine the flour and sugar in a large mixing bowl. Grate the butter into the flour. Add the grated cheese and stir to coat the cheese and butter with flour. Then add the buttermilk and stir just until you can no longer see streaks of flour. The dough should be quite wet.

3. Spread the all-purpose (not self-rising) flour out on a small cookie sheet. With a spoon, scoop 8 evenly sized balls of dough into the flour, making sure they don't touch each other. With floured hands, coat each dough ball with flour and toss them gently from hand to hand to stir any excess flour. Place each floured dough ball into the prepared pan, right up next to the other. This will help the biscuits rise up, rather than spreading out.

4. Preheat the toaster oven to 380°F.

5. Transfer the cake pan to the air fryer oven, lowering it into the air fryer oven using a sling made of aluminum foil (fold a piece of aluminum foil into a strip about 2-inches wide by 24-inches long). Let the ends of the aluminum foil sling hang across the cake pan before returning to the air fryer oven.

6. Air-fry for 20 minutes. Check the biscuits a couple of times to make sure they are not getting too brown on top. If they are, re-arrange the aluminum foil strips to cover any brown parts. After 20 minutes, check the biscuits by inserting a toothpick into the center of the biscuits. It should come out clean. If it needs a little more time, continue to air-fry for a couple of extra minutes. Brush the tops of the biscuits with some melted butter and sprinkle a little more grated cheese on top if desired. Air-fry for another 2 minutes. Remove the cake pan from the air fryer oven using the aluminum sling. Let the biscuits cool for just a minute or two and then turn them out onto a plate and pull apart. Serve immediately.

French Toast Casserole

Servings: 6
Cooking Time: 60 Minutes

Ingredients:
- 1 tablespoon unsalted butter, softened, plus 6 tablespoons unsalted butter, melted, divided
- ¾ cup packed (5¼ ounces) brown sugar
- 1 tablespoon ground cinnamon
- ½ teaspoon ground nutmeg
- ⅛ teaspoon table salt
- 18 slices potato sandwich bread, divided
- 2½ cups whole milk
- 6 large eggs
- ¼ cup sliced almonds, toasted
- Confectioners' sugar

Directions:
1. Adjust toaster oven rack to middle position and preheat the toaster oven to 350 degrees. Grease 13 by 9-inch baking dish with softened butter. Mix brown sugar, cinnamon, nutmeg, and salt together in bowl.

2. Sprinkle 3 tablespoons brown sugar mixture evenly over bottom of prepared dish. Place 6 bread slices (use bread heels here) in even layer in bottom of dish. Brush bread with 1½ tablespoons melted butter and sprinkle with 3 tablespoons sugar mixture.

3. Place 6 bread slices in single layer over first layer, brush with 1½ tablespoons melted butter, then sprinkle with 3 tablespoons sugar mixture. Place remaining 6 bread slices over previous layer and brush with 1½ tablespoons melted butter.

4. In separate bowl, whisk milk and eggs until well combined, then pour evenly over bread.

Gently press down on layers with spatula to saturate bread. (Casserole can be covered and refrigerated for up to 12 hours.)

5. Sprinkle with almonds and remaining sugar mixture. Bake until casserole is slightly puffed and golden brown and bubbling around edges, 30 to 35 minutes, rotating dish halfway through baking. Transfer dish to wire rack, brush with remaining 1½ tablespoons melted butter, and let cool for 15 minutes. Sprinkle with confectioners' sugar and serve.

French Toast Sticks

Servings: 4
Cooking Time: 8 Minutes

Ingredients:
- 2 eggs
- ¼ cup half-and-half
- ½ teaspoon vanilla extract
- 6 slices wheat bread, cut into 1-inch strips
- 1 teaspoon ground cinnamon
- 2 tablespoons granulated sugar
- Maple syrup or pureed strawberries for serving

Directions:
1. In an 8-x-12-inch casserole dish, whisk together the eggs, half-and-half, and vanilla. Lay the strips of bread into the baking dish and flip around. Allow the bread to soak up the egg mixture for 10 minutes.
2. Meanwhile, in a small bowl, stir together the cinnamon and sugar.
3. Place the soaked bread strips into the air fryer oven, not touching one another. Spray with cooking spray and sprinkle the cinnamon and sugar mixture onto the bread sticks.

4. Air fry the French toast sticks at 370°F for 8 minutes. Cook in batches, as needed.
5. Serve with maple syrup or pureed strawberries

Broiled Bananas

Servings: 2
Cooking Time: 10 Minutes

Ingredients:
- Sauce:
- 1 tablespoon margarine
- 2 tablespoons honey
- 2 tablespoons lemon juice
- Pinch of salt (optional)
- 2 bananas, peeled, halved and quartered
- Creamy Yogurt Sauce or fat-free half-and-half

Directions:
1. Place the sauce ingredients in an oiled or nonstick 8½ × 8½ × 2-inch square baking (cake) pan.
2. BROIL for 5 minutes, or until the mixture begins to bubble. Remove the pan carefully from the oven using oven mitts and stir to blend. Add the bananas and spoon the sauce over them.
3. BROIL for 5 minutes, or until the bananas are tender and golden in color.
4. Place 4 banana quarters each in 2 dessert dishes and spoon equal portions of the sauce over them. Serve with Creamy Yogurt Sauce or drizzle with fat-free half-and-half.

Baked Parmesan Eggs

Servings: 4
Cooking Time: 10 Minutes

Ingredients:
- 4 large eggs, each cracked into a small 1-cup baking dish

- 4 tablespoons grated Parmesan cheese
- 4 tablespoons fat-free half-and-half
- Salt and freshly ground black pepper

Directions:

1. Preheat the toaster oven to 400° F.
2. Top each egg with 1 tablespoon Parmesan cheese and 1 tablespoon half-and-half. Season to taste with salt and pepper and add any preferred additions.
3. BAKE for 10 minutes, or to your preference, testing the eggs by touching the surface with a spoon for the desired firmness after 5 minutes.

Espresso Chip Muffins

Servings: 6
Cooking Time: 20 Minutes

Ingredients:

- 1 cup all-purpose flour
- 6 tablespoons packed dark brown sugar
- 1 ¼ teaspoons baking powder
- 1 teaspoon instant espresso coffee powder
- ¼ teaspoon table salt
- ¼ teaspoon ground cinnamon
- ½ cup whole milk
- ¼ cup unsalted butter, melted and cooled slightly
- 1 large egg
- ½ teaspoon pure vanilla extract
- ½ cup mini semisweet chocolate chips

Directions:

1. Preheat the toaster oven to 375°F. Grease a 6-cup muffin pan.
2. Whisk the flour, brown sugar, baking powder, espresso, salt, and cinnamon in a medium bowl. Combine the milk, butter, egg, and vanilla in a small bowl until blended. Make a well in the center of the flour mixture and add the milk

mixture. Stir until just combined. Fold in the chocolate chips.
3. Spoon the batter evenly into the prepared muffin cups. Bake for 18 to 20 minutes, or until a wooden pick inserted into the center comes out clean. Cool on a wire rack for 5 minutes, then remove the muffins from the pan to finish cooling on a wire rack. Serve warm or at room temperature. Store in an airtight container.

Breakfast Blueberry Peach Crisp

Servings: 8
Cooking Time: 60 Minutes

Ingredients:

- Filling Ingredients
- 4 cups blueberries, fresh or frozen
- 2 cups peaches, sliced
- 1 teaspoon vanilla extract
- 2 teaspoons lemon juice
- 4 tablespoons pure maple syrup
- 1½ tablespoons cornstarch
- A tiny pinch of salt
- Topping Ingredients
- 2½ cups rolled oats
- 5 tablespoons almond meal (or almond flour)
- 1 teaspoon cinnamon
- 5 tablespoons pure maple syrup
- 3 tablespoons coconut sugar (or brown sugar)
- 7 tablespoons coconut oil, melted
- 1 cup sliced almonds
- 1 cup chopped walnuts
- ¼ teaspoon salt

Directions:

1. Combine the blueberries, peaches, vanilla extract, lemon juice, maple syrup, cornstarch, and salt in a bowl and toss to combine. Pour mixture into the baking dish.

2. Combine all the topping ingredients in a separate bowl and stir until clumps form, then spread evenly over the fruit mixture.

3. Preheat the toaster Oven to 350°F.

4. Place the baking dish on the wire rack, then insert rack at low position in the preheated oven.

5. Select the Bake function, adjust time to 1 hour, then press

6. Start/Pause.

7. Remove crisp when golden on top and fruit is bubbly.

8. Serve with yogurt for breakfast or vanilla ice cream for dessert.

Stromboli

Servings: 4
Cooking Time: 30 Minutes

Ingredients:
- CRUST
- 2 cups all-purpose flour
- 2 tablespoons unsalted butter, cut into small pieces
- 1 teaspoon table salt
- 2 teaspoons active dry yeast
- 2 teaspoons sugar
- TOPPINGS
- ½ cup marinara or pizza sauce
- ½ teaspoon Italian seasoning
- 2 ounces pepperoni slices
- 2 ounces salami slices
- 2 ounces thin ham slices
- 1 ½ cups shredded mozzarella cheese
- 3 tablespoons shredded Parmesan cheese
- 1 large egg
- ½ teaspoon granulated garlic
- 1 teaspoon sesame seeds

Directions:

1. Make the crust: Place the flour in a large bowl and create a well. Place ⅔ cup water, the butter and salt in a small microwave-safe bowl and microwave on High (100 percent) power for 30 seconds or until warm. (The temperature of the mixture should not be above 110 °F.) Pour the liquid into the well. Sprinkle the yeast and sugar over the water mixture and allow to stand for 5 minutes. Mix the flour mixture until a dough forms. Oil a medium bowl and place the dough in the bowl. Cover and let rise for 1 hour.

2. Preheat the toaster oven to 375 °F. Line a 12 x 12-inch baking pan with parchment paper.

3. Flour a clean surface and roll the dough into a 15 x 13 ½-inch rectangle. Place the dough diagonally on the prepared pan. Spread the marinara sauce over the surface of the dough to within ½ inch of all four edges. Sprinkle with the Italian seasoning. Layer the pepperoni, salami, and ham slices on top of the marinara. Sprinkle with the cheeses. Roll up as tightly as possible and pinch the seams to make sure nothings seeps out.

4. Whisk the egg, 1 tablespoon of water, and the garlic in a small bowl. Brush the egg wash over the stromboli and sprinkle with the sesame seeds. Bake for 25 to 30 minutes or until golden brown.

Pecan-topped Baked Oatmeal

Servings: 6
Cooking Time: 45 Minutes

Ingredients:
- 2 tablespoons unsalted butter, plus additional for the pan
- 2 large eggs
- 3 cups whole milk
- ¼ cup packed dark brown sugar

- 1 teaspoon ground cinnamon
- 1 teaspoon pure vanilla extract
- ¼ teaspoon kosher salt
- 3 cups old-fashioned oats
- TOPPING
- ¼ cup packed dark brown sugar
- ½ cup chopped pecans
- Fresh blueberries (optional)
- Milk (optional)

Directions:

1. Lightly butter an 8 x 8-inch square baking pan.

2. Melt 2 tablespoons butter; set aside to cool slightly.

3. Whisk the eggs in a large bowl. Add the milk, brown sugar, cinnamon, vanilla, and salt and whisk to combine. Stir in the oats. Stir in the melted butter. Pour into the prepared pan. Cover and refrigerate overnight.

4. When ready to bake, preheat the toaster oven to 350°F. Gently stir the oat mixture in the baking pan.

5. Make the topping: Blend the brown sugar and pecans in a small bowl. Sprinkle the pecan mixture over the top of the oats. Bake, uncovered, for 40 to 45 minutes or until it is set and a knife inserted in the center comes out clean.

6. Sprinkle with fresh blueberries, if desired. Spoon into bowls and serve with milk to drizzle on top.

Apple Maple Pudding

Servings: 4
Cooking Time: 20 Minutes

Ingredients:
- Pudding mixture:
- 2 eggs

- ½ cup brown sugar
- 4 tablespoons maple syrup
- 3 tablespoons unbleached flour
- 1 teaspoon baking powder
- 1 teaspoon vanilla extract
- ¼ cup chopped raisins
- ¼ cup chopped walnuts
- 2 medium apples, peeled and chopped

Directions:

1. Preheat the toaster oven to 350° F.

2. Combine the pudding mixture ingredients in a medium bowl, beating the eggs, sugar, and maple syrup together first, then adding the flour, baking powder, and vanilla. Add the raisins, nuts, and apples and mix thoroughly. Pour into an oiled or nonstick 8½ × 8½ × 2-inch square baking (cake) pan.

3. BAKE for 20 minutes, or until a toothpick inserted in the center comes out clean.

4. BROIL for 5 minutes, or until the top is lightly browned.

Oatmeal Piecrust

Servings: 4
Cooking Time: 20 Minutes

Ingredients:
- 2 cups quick-cooking rolled oats
- 3 tablespoons margarine
- 1 tablespoon vegetable oil
- ½ cup confectioners' sugar
- Salt to taste

Directions:

1. Preheat the toaster oven to 350° F.

2. Combine all the ingredients with a fork in a medium bowl, blending well and adding a little water if the mixture is too crumbly.

3. Press the mixture into a 9¾-inch round pie pan. The crust must be even in thickness.

4. BAKE for 20 minutes, or until the crust is lightly browned. Cool before filling.

Mahi Mahi Tacos With Pineapple Salsa

Servings: 2
Cooking Time: 9 Minutes

Ingredients:
- Salsa Ingredients
- 1 cup pineapple, diced
- ½ lime, zested and juiced
- 1 small jalapeno, diced
- 1 avocado, diced
- ¼ red onion, diced
- 2 tablespoons cilantro, chopped
- A pinch of salt
- Mahi Mahi Ingredients
- 2 (6-ounce) filets of Mahi Mahi fish
- 1 tablespoon olive oil
- Salt & pepper, to taste
- Corn tortillas for serving

Directions:
1. Combine all the salsa ingredients in a bowl. Stir together and taste, then add additional salt if desired. Store salsa in the fridge until ready to serve.

2. Preheat the toaster Oven to 430°F.

3. Line the food tray with foil, then place mahi mahi on the tray. Drizzle with olive oil and season with salt and pepper.

4. Insert food tray at top position in the preheated oven.

5. Select the Air Fry function, adjust time to 9 minutes, and press Start/Pause.

6. Remove when the internal temperature of the mahi mahi reaches close to 145°F. Allow fish to rest for 5 minutes, then flake into large pieces.

7. Assemble tacos by placing pieces of mahi mahi onto warmed corn tortillas. Top with salsa and serve.

Cherries Jubilee

Servings: 4
Cooking Time: 10 Minutes

Ingredients:
- 1 15-ounce can cherries, pitted and drained, with 2 tablespoons juice reserved
- 1 tablespoon orange juice
- 1 tablespoon sugar
- 1 tablespoon cornstarch
- ¼ cup warmed Kirsch or Cognac
- Vanilla yogurt or fat-free half-and-half

Directions:
1. Combine the reserved juice, orange juice, sugar, and cornstarch in a shallow baking pan, blending well.

2. BROIL for 5 minutes, or until the juice clarifies and thickens slightly. Add the cherries and heat, broiling for 5 minutes more and stirring to blend. Remove from the oven and transfer to a flameproof serving dish.

3. Spoon the Kirsch over the cherries and ignite. Top with vanilla yogurt or drizzle with warm fat-free half-and-half and serve.

Nacho Chips

Servings: 12
Cooking Time: 20 Minutes

Ingredients:
- 3 jalapeño peppers
- 4 6-inch flour tortillas

- 1 cup shredded low-fat Cheddar cheese

Directions:

1. Seed and cut the jalapeño peppers into thin rings. Arrange one-fourth of the rings on the tortilla. It's a good idea to wear gloves, since the peppers can sometimes cause skin irritation.
2. Place the tortilla in an oiled or nonstick 8½ × 8½ × 2-inch square baking (cake) pan. Sprinkle evenly with ¼ cup cheese.
3. BROIL for 5 minutes, or until the cheese is melted. Repeat the process for the remaining tortillas. Cut each into 6 wedges with a sharp knife or scissors.

Oven-baked Reuben

Servings: 2
Cooking Time: 3 Minutes

Ingredients:

- 4 slices rye bread
- 2 tablespoons Dijon mustard
- 6 slices reduced-fat Swiss cheese
- 1 6-ounce package sliced corned beef
- ½ cup sauerkraut, drained
- Russian Dressing (recipe follows)

Directions:

1. Spread each slice of bread with mustard. Layer 2 slices with 3 slices each of Swiss cheese and equal portions of corned beef and sauerkraut. Top with the remaining bread slices and place on a broiling rack with the pan underneath.
2. TOAST twice, or until the cheese is melted. Serve with Russian Dressing.

Oat Bran Muffins

Servings: 8
Cooking Time: 12 Minutes

Ingredients:

- ⅔ cup oat bran
- ½ cup flour
- ¼ cup brown sugar
- 1 teaspoon baking powder
- ½ teaspoon baking soda
- ⅛ teaspoon salt
- ½ cup buttermilk
- 1 egg
- 2 tablespoons canola oil
- ½ cup chopped dates, raisins, or dried cranberries
- 24 paper muffin cups
- cooking spray

Directions:

1. Preheat the toaster oven to 330°F.
2. In a large bowl, combine the oat bran, flour, brown sugar, baking powder, baking soda, and salt.
3. In a small bowl, beat together the buttermilk, egg, and oil.
4. Pour buttermilk mixture into bowl with dry ingredients and stir just until moistened. Do not beat.
5. Gently stir in dried fruit.
6. Use triple baking cups to help muffins hold shape during baking. Spray them with cooking spray, place 4 sets of cups in air fryer oven at a time, and fill each one ¾ full of batter.
7. Air-fry for 12 minutes, until top springs back when lightly touched and toothpick inserted in center comes out clean.
8. Repeat for remaining muffins.

Toasted Cheese Sandwich

Servings: 1
Cooking Time: 8 Minutes

Ingredients:

- 2 slices bread, country, sourdough, white, or your choice
- 2 teaspoons salted butter, softened
- 2 to 3 slices cheese such as Colby Jack or cheddar

Directions:

1. Place a baking pan into the toaster oven and preheat with the baking pan in the oven to 450°F (not the Toast setting).
2. Spread one side of each slice of bread with the butter. Place one piece of bread, buttered side down, on a plate and top with the cheese slices. (Do not allow any cheese to hang over the edge of the bread.) Top with the second slice bread, buttered side up.
3. Carefully remove the hot baking pan from the toaster oven and place the sandwich in the middle of the pan. Bake for 4 minutes. Carefully remove the pan and flip the sandwich, using a spatula. Bake for an additional 3 to 4 minutes, or until the sandwich is golden brown and the cheese is melted.
4. Cool slightly and cut in half for serving.

Lemon Blueberry Scones

Servings: 6
Cooking Time: 25 Minutes

Ingredients:

- 1 ½ cups all-purpose flour
- 2 tablespoons granulated sugar
- 2 ¼ teaspoons baking powder
- 1 teaspoon grated lemon zest
- ¼ teaspoon table salt
- ¼ cup unsalted butter, cut into 1-tablespoon pieces
- ¾ cup fresh or frozen blueberries
- ¾ cup plus 1 tablespoon heavy cream, plus more for brushing
- Coarse white sugar
- LEMON GLAZE
- 1 cup confectioners' sugar
- 2 to 3 tablespoons fresh lemon juice

Directions:

1. Line a 12 x 12-inch baking pan with parchment paper.
2. Whisk the flour, granulated sugar, baking powder, lemon zest, and salt in a large bowl. Cut in the butter using a pastry cutter or two knives until the mixture is crumbly throughout. Gently stir in the blueberries, taking care not to mash them. Add ¾ cup cream and gently stir until a soft dough forms. If needed, stir in an additional tablespoon of cream so all of the flour is moistened.
3. Turn the dough onto a lightly floured board. Pat the dough into a circle about ¾ inch thick and 6 inches in diameter. Cut into 6 triangles. Arrange the triangles on the prepared pan. Freeze for 15 minutes.
4. Preheat the toaster oven to 400°F. Brush the scones lightly with cream and sprinkle with coarse sugar. Bake for 20 to 25 minutes or until golden brown. Let cool for 5 minutes.
5. Meanwhile, make the glaze: Stir the confectioners' sugar and lemon juice in a small bowl, blending until smooth. Drizzle the glaze over the scones. Let stand for about 5 minutes. These taste best served freshly made and slightly warm.

Apple Fritters

Servings: 6
Cooking Time: 12 Minutes

Ingredients:

- 1 cup all-purpose flour
- 1½ teaspoons baking powder
- ¼ teaspoon salt
- 2 tablespoon brown sugar
- 1 teaspoon vanilla extract
- ¾ cup plain Greek yogurt
- 1 tablespoon cinnamon
- 1 large Granny Smith apple, cored, peeled, and finely chopped
- ¼ cup chopped walnuts
- ½ cup powdered sugar
- 1 tablespoon milk

Directions:

1. Preheat the toaster oven to 320°F.
2. In a medium bowl, combine the flour, baking powder, and salt.
3. In a large bowl, add the brown sugar, vanilla, yogurt, cinnamon, apples, and walnuts. Mix the dry ingredients into the wet, using your hands to combine, until all the ingredients are mixed together. Knead the mixture in the bowl about 4 times.
4. Lightly spray the air fryer oven with olive oil spray.
5. Divide the batter into 6 equally sized balls; then lightly flatten them and place inside the air fryer oven. Repeat until all the fritters are formed.
6. Place in the air fryer oven and air-fry for 6 minutes, flip, and then cook another 6 minutes.
7. While the fritters are cooking, in a small bowl, mix the powdered sugar with the milk. Set aside.
8. When the cooking completes, remove the air fryer oven and allow the fritters to cool on a wire rack. Drizzle with the homemade glaze and serve.

Sheet-pan Hash Browns

Servings: 2
Cooking Time: 60 Minutes

Ingredients:

- 1½ pounds Yukon Gold potatoes, unpeeled, shredded
- 3 tablespoons extra-virgin olive oil
- ½ teaspoon table salt
- ⅛ teaspoon pepper

Directions:

1. Adjust toaster oven rack to lowest position, select air-fry or convection function, and preheat the toaster oven to 450 degrees. Place potatoes in large bowl and cover with cold water. Let sit for 5 minutes.
2. Lift potatoes out of water, one handful at a time, and transfer to colander; discard water. Rinse and dry bowl. Place half of shredded potatoes in center of clean dish towel. Gather ends of towel and twist tightly to wring out excess moisture from potatoes. Transfer dried potatoes to now-empty bowl. Repeat with remaining potatoes.
3. Add oil, salt, and pepper to potatoes and toss to combine. Distribute potatoes in even layer on small rimmed baking sheet, but do not pack down. Cook until top of potatoes is spotty brown, 30 to 40 minutes, rotating sheet halfway through baking.
4. Remove sheet from oven. Using spatula, flip hash browns in sections. Return sheet to oven and continue to cook until spotty brown and dry, 10 to 15 minutes. Season with salt and pepper to taste. Serve.

Breakfast Banana Bread

Servings: 6
Cooking Time: 40 Minutes

Ingredients:

- 2 ripe bananas
- 1 egg
- ½ cup skim milk
- 2 tablespoons honey
- 1 tablespoon vegetable oil
- 1 cup unbleached flour
- ¾ cup chopped trail mix
- 1 teaspoon baking powder
- Salt

Directions:

1. Preheat the toaster oven to 400° F.
2. Process the bananas, egg, milk, honey, and oil in a blender or food processor until smooth and transfer to a mixing bowl.
3. Add the flour and trail mix, stirring to mix well. Add the baking powder and stir just enough to blend it into the batter. Add salt to taste. Pour the mixture into an oiled or nonstick 4½ × 8½ × 2¼-inch loaf pan.
4. BAKE for 40 minutes, or until a toothpick inserted in the center comes out clean.

Western Frittata

Servings: 1
Cooking Time: 19 Minutes

Ingredients:

- ½ red or green bell pepper, cut into ½-inch chunks
- 1 teaspoon olive oil
- 3 eggs, beaten
- ¼ cup grated Cheddar cheese
- ¼ cup diced cooked ham
- salt and freshly ground black pepper, to taste
- 1 teaspoon butter
- 1 teaspoon chopped fresh parsley

Directions:

1. Preheat the toaster oven to 400°F.
2. Toss the peppers with the olive oil and air-fry for 6 minutes, redistribute the ingredients once or twice during the process.
3. While the vegetables are cooking, beat the eggs well in a bowl, stir in the Cheddar cheese and ham, and season with salt and freshly ground black pepper. Add the air-fried peppers to this bowl when they have finished cooking.
4. Place a 6- or 7-inch non-stick metal cake pan into the air fryer oven with the butter using an aluminum sling to lower the pan into the air fryer oven. (Fold a piece of aluminum foil into a strip about 2-inches wide by 24-inches long.) Air-fry for 1 minute at 380°F to melt the butter. Remove the cake pan and rotate the pan to distribute the butter and grease the pan. Pour the egg mixture into the cake pan and return the pan to the air fryer oven, using the aluminum sling.
5. Air-fry at 380°F for 12 minutes, or until the frittata has puffed up and is lightly browned. Let the frittata sit in the air fryer oven for 5 minutes to cool to an edible temperature and set up. Remove the cake pan from the air fryer oven, sprinkle with parsley and serve immediately.

Almond Cranberry Granola

Servings: 12
Cooking Time: 9 Minutes

Ingredients:

- 2 tablespoons sesame seeds
- ¼ cup chopped almonds
- ¼ cup sunflower seeds

- ½ cup unsweetened shredded coconut
- 2 tablespoons unsalted butter, melted or at least softened
- 2 tablespoons coconut oil
- ⅓ cup honey
- 2½ cups oats
- ¼ teaspoon sea salt
- ½ cup dried cranberries

Directions:

1. In a large mixing bowl, stir together the sesame seeds, almonds, sunflower seeds, coconut, butter, coconut oil, honey, oats, and salt.

2. Line the air fryer oven with parchment paper. Punch 8 to 10 holes into the parchment paper with a fork so air can circulate. Pour the granola mixture onto the parchment paper.

3. Air fry the granola at 350°F for 9 minutes, stirring every 3 minutes.

4. When cooking is complete, stir in the dried cranberries and allow the mixture to cool. Store in an airtight container up to 2 weeks or freeze for 6 months.

Onion And Cheese Buttermilk Biscuits

Servings: 4
Cooking Time: 15 Minutes

Ingredients:

- 2 cups unbleached flour
- 3 tablespoons margarine, at room temperature
- ¾ cup low-fat buttermilk
- 4 teaspoons baking powder
- 1 teaspoon garlic powder
- ¼ cup grated Parmesan cheese
- 3 tablespoons finely chopped onion
- 2 tablespoons chopped fresh parsley
- Salt to taste

Directions:

1. Preheat the toaster oven to 400° F.

2. Blend all the ingredients in a medium bowl with a fork, then press together to form a dough ball.

3. KNEAD the dough on a lightly floured surface just until smooth.

4. Roll the dough to ½-inch thickness and cut with a round 3-inch cookie cutter. Place on an oiled or nonstick 6½ × 10-inch baking sheet or in an oiled or nonstick 8½ × 8½ × 2-inch square baking (cake) pan.

5. BAKE for 15 minutes, or until lightly browned.

Morning Glory Muffins

Servings: 6
Cooking Time: 25 Minutes

Ingredients:

- Oil spray (hand-pumped)
- ¼ cup raisins
- 1 cup whole-wheat flour
- ½ cup packed dark brown sugar
- 1 teaspoon baking soda
- 1¼ teaspoons pumpkin pie spice
- ¼ teaspoon sea salt
- 1 cup carrot, finely shredded
- 1 small apple, peeled, cored, and shredded
- ⅓ cup shredded, sweetened coconut
- 2 large eggs
- ¼ cup canola oil
- Juice and zest of ½ orange

Directions:

1. Place the rack on position 1 and preheat the toaster oven on BAKE to 350°F for 5 minutes. Lightly spray 6 muffin cups with the oil or line them with paper liners.

2. In a small bowl, cover the raisins with hot water and set aside.

3. In a large bowl, whisk the flour, brown sugar, baking soda, pumpkin pie spice, and salt. Add the carrot, apple, and coconut, and toss to mix.

4. In a small bowl, beat the eggs, oil, orange juice, and orange zest.

5. Drain the raisins, squeezing out as much water as possible.

6. Add the wet ingredients and raisins to the dry ingredients and mix until the batter is just combined.

7. Spoon the batter into the muffin cups.

8. Bake for 25 minutes or until a knife inserted in the center comes out clean.

9. Remove from the oven and let cool before serving.

Strawberry Shortcake With Buttermilk Biscuits

Servings: 8
Cooking Time: 15 Minutes

Ingredients:
- 1 quart fresh strawberries, rinsed and sliced
- 2 tablespoons sugar
- 1 tablespoon lemon juice
- Buttermilk biscuit mix:
- 2 cups unbleached flour
- 2 teaspoons baking powder
- ½ teaspoon baking soda
- Salt to taste
- ¼ cup margarine
- 1 cup low-fat buttermilk
- Vegetable oil
- Nonfat whipped topping

Directions:
1. Preheat the toaster oven to 400° F.

2. Combine the strawberries, sugar, and lemon juice in a large bowl, mixing well to blend. Set aside.

3. Combine the flour, baking powder, baking soda, and salt in a large bowl. Add the margarine, cutting it into the flour with a knife or pastry cutter. Add just enough buttermilk so that the dough will hold together when pinched.

4. Turn the dough out onto a lightly floured surface and knead 5 or 6 times. Drop the dough from a tablespoon onto an oiled or nonstick 6½ × 10-inch baking sheet. Make 8 mounds 1½ inches across and flatten the tops with a spoon.

5. BAKE for 15 minutes, or until the biscuits are lightly browned. Cool. Spoon on the fresh strawberries. Top with nonfat whipped topping and serve.

LUNCH AND DINNER

Glazed Pork Tenderloin With Carrots Sheet Pan Supper

Servings: 4-6
Cooking Time: 20 Minutes

Ingredients:

- 1 pound pork tenderloin
- 1 teaspoon steak seasoning blend
- 2 large carrots, sliced 1/2-inch thick
- 2 large parsnips, sliced 1/2-inch thick
- 1/2 small sweet onion, cut in thin wedges
- 1 tablespoon olive oil
- Salt and pepper to taste
- 1/2 cup apricot jam
- 1 tablespoon balsamic vinegar

Directions:

1. Place rack on bottom position of toaster oven. Heat the toaster oven to 425°F. Spray the toaster oven baking pan with nonstick cooking spray or line the pan with nonstick aluminum foil.
2. Place pork tenderloin diagonally in center of pan. Sprinkle pork with seasoning blend.
3. In a large bowl, combine carrots, parsnips and onion. Add olive oil, salt and black pepper and stir until vegetables are coated. Arrange vegetables evenly in pan around pork.
4. Bake 20 minutes. Stir vegetables.
5. Meanwhile, in a small bowl, combine apricot jam and balsamic vinegar. Spoon about half of mixture over pork.
6. Continue baking until pork reaches reaches 160°F when tested with a meat thermometer and vegetables are roasted, about 10 minutes. Slice pork and serve with remaining sauce, if desired.

Connecticut Garden Chowder

Servings: 4
Cooking Time: 60 Minutes

Ingredients:

- Soup:
- ½ cup peeled and shredded potato
- ½ cup shredded carrot
- ½ cup shredded celery 2 plum tomatoes, chopped
- 1 small zucchini, shredded
- 2 bay leaves
- ¼ teaspoon sage
- 1 teaspoon garlic powder
- Salt and butcher's pepper to taste
- Chowder base:
- 2 tablespoons reduced-fat cream cheese, at room temperature
- ½ cup fat-free half-and-half
- 2 tablespoons unbleached flour
- 2 tablespoons chopped fresh parsley

Directions:

1. Preheat the toaster oven to 375° F.
2. Combine the soup ingredients in a 1-quart 8½ × 8½ × 4-inch ovenproof baking dish, mixing well. Adjust the seasonings to taste.
3. BAKE, covered, for 40 minutes, or until the vegetables are tender.
4. Whisk the chowder mixture ingredients together until smooth. Add the mixture to the cooked soup ingredients and stir well to blend.
5. BAKE, uncovered for 20 minutes, or until the stock is thickened. Ladle the soup into individual soup bowls and garnish with the parsley.

Baked French Toast With Maple Bourbon Syrup

Servings: 6
Cooking Time: 40 Minutes

Ingredients:

- Nonstick cooking spray
- 4 tablespoons unsalted butter, melted
- ½ cup packed dark brown sugar
- ⅔ cup chopped pecans, toasted
- 6 (1-inch-thick) slices crusty artisan, brioche, or firm country bread
- 3 large eggs
- 1 cup milk
- 1 teaspoon pure vanilla extract
- ⅓ cup maple syrup
- 2 tablespoons bourbon

Directions:

1. Spray an 11 x 7 x 2 ½-inch baking dish with nonstick cooking spray. Pour the butter into the dish. Stir in the brown sugar and pecans. Arrange the bread at an angle in the dish, overlapping the bottom of the slices as necessary.

2. Whisk the eggs, milk, and vanilla in a medium bowl. Drizzle the milk mixture over the bread, taking care to pour slowly and moisten the edges of the bread. Cover and refrigerate overnight.

3. When ready to bake, preheat the toaster oven to 350°F. Bake, uncovered, for 30 to 35 minutes or until golden and set.

4. Mix the maple syrup and bourbon in a small bowl. Drizzle the syrup over the French toast. Bake for 3 to 5 minutes. Let stand for 2 to 3 minutes, then serve warm.

Healthy Southwest Stuffed Peppers

Servings: 6
Cooking Time: 30 Minutes

Ingredients:

- 1 tablespoon oil
- 1 small onion, chopped
- 1 garlic clove, minced
- 1/2 pound ground turkey
- 1/2 cup drained black beans
- 1/2 cup whole kernel corn
- 1 jar (16 oz.) medium salsa, divided
- 1/2 cup cooked white rice
- 1/2 teaspoon chili powder
- 1/2 teaspoon salt
- 1/4 teaspoon ground cumin
- 1/4 teaspoon black pepper
- 3 medium peppers, halved lengthwise leaving stem on, seeded
- 1/3 cup shredded Monterey Jack cheese, divided
- Sour cream
- Chopped fresh cilantro

Directions:

1. Preheat the toaster oven to 350°F. Spray baking pan with nonstick cooking spray.

2. In a large skillet over medium-high, heat oil. Add onion and garlic, cook for 2 to 3 minutes.

3. Add turkey to skillet, cook, stirring frequently, for 6 to 8 minutes or until turkey is cooked through.

4. Stir black beans, corn, 1/2 cup salsa, rice, chili powder, salt, cumin and pepper into turkey mixture.

5. Fill each pepper half with turkey mixture, dividing mixture evenly among peppers.

6. Top each pepper half with remaining salsa.
7. Bake 20 minutes. Sprinkle with cheese and bake an additional 10 minutes or until heated through.
8. Top with sour cream and cilantro.

Tarragon Beef Ragout

Servings: 6
Cooking Time: 53 Minutes

Ingredients:
- 1 pound lean round steak, cut across the grain of the meat into thin strips, approximately ¼ × 2 inches
- ½ cup dry red wine
- 1 small onion, chopped
- 2 carrots, peeled and thinly sliced
- 3 2 plum tomatoes, chopped
- 1 celery stalk, chopped
- 1 10-ounce package frozen peas
- 3 garlic gloves, minced
- 1 tablespoon Dijon mustard
- ½ teaspoon ground cumin
- ½ teaspoon dried tarragon
- Salt and freshly ground black pepper to taste

Directions:
1. Preheat the toaster oven to 375° F.
2. Combine all the ingredients with ½ cup water in an 8½ × 8½ × 4-inch ovenproof baking dish. Adjust the seasonings. Cover with aluminum foil.
3. BAKE, covered, for 45 minutes, or until the beef, onion, and celery are tender. Remove the cover.
4. BROIL 8 minutes to reduce the liquid and lightly brown the top.

Miso-glazed Salmon With Broccoli

Servings: 2
Cooking Time: 25 Minutes

Ingredients:
- Nonstick cooking spray
- 2 tablespoons miso, preferably yellow
- 2 tablespoons mirin
- 1 tablespoon packed dark brown sugar
- 2 teaspoons minced fresh ginger
- 1 ½ teaspoons sesame oil
- 8 ounces fresh broccoli, cut into spears
- 1 tablespoon canola or vegetable oil
- Kosher salt and freshly ground black pepper
- 2 salmon fillets (5 to 6 ounces each)

Directions:
1. Preheat the toaster oven to 425°F. Spray a 12 x 12-inch baking pan with nonstick cooking spray.
2. Stir the miso, mirin, brown sugar, ginger, and sesame oil in a small bowl; set aside.
3. Toss the broccoli spears with the canola oil and season with salt and pepper. Place the broccoli on the pan. Bake, uncovered, for 10 minutes. Stir the broccoli and move to one side of the pan.
4. Place the salmon, skin side down, on the other end of the pan. Brush lightly with olive oil and season with salt and pepper. Bake for 10 minutes.
5. Brush the fish generously with the miso sauce. Bake for an additional 3 to 5 minutes, or until the fish flakes easily with a fork and a meat thermometer registers 145°F.

Roasted Vegetable Gazpacho

Servings: 4
Cooking Time: 35 Minutes

Ingredients:

- Vegetables and seasonings:
- 1 bell pepper, thinly sliced
- ½ cup chopped celery
- ½ cup frozen or canned corn
- 1 medium onion, thinly sliced
- 1 small yellow squash, cut into 1-inch slices
- 1 small zucchini, cut into 1-inch slices
- 3 garlic cloves, chopped
- ½ teaspoon ground cumin
- 2 tablespoons olive oil
- Salt and freshly ground black pepper to taste
- 1 quart tomato juice
- 1 tablespoon lemon juice
- 3 tablespoons chopped fresh cilantro

Directions:

1. Preheat the toaster oven to 400°F.
2. Combine the vegetables and seasonings in an oiled or nonstick 8½ × 8½ × 2-inch square baking (cake) pan, mixing well.
3. BAKE, covered, for 25 minutes, or until the onions and celery are tender. Remove from the oven, uncover, and turn the vegetable pieces with tongs.
4. BROIL for 10 minutes, or until the vegetables are lightly browned. Remove from the oven and cool. Transfer to a large nonaluminum container and add the tomato juice, lemon juice, and cilantro. Adjust the seasonings.
5. Chill, covered, for several hours, preferably a day or two to enrich the flavor of the stock.

Baked Parsleyed Cheese Grits

Servings: 4

Cooking Time: 30 Minutes

Ingredients:

- 4 strips lean uncooked turkey bacon, cut in half
- 1 cup grits
- 2 cups skim or low-fat soy milk
- 1 egg
- ½ cup shredded Parmesan cheese
- 1 tablespoon chopped fresh parsley
- ½ teaspoon garlic powder
- Salt and butcher's pepper to taste

Directions:

1. Preheat the toaster oven to 350° F.
2. Layer an 8½ × 8½ × 2-inch square baking (cake) pan with the bacon strips.
3. Combine the remaining ingredients in a medium bowl and pour the mixture over the strips.
4. BAKE, uncovered, for 30 minutes, or until the grits are cooked. Cut into squares with a spatula and serve.

Oven-baked Barley

Servings: 2
Cooking Time: 60 Minutes

Ingredients:

- ⅓ cup barley, toasted
- Seasonings:
- 1 tablespoon sesame oil
- 1 tablespoon sesame seeds
- ¼ teaspoon ground cumin
- ¼ teaspoon turmeric
- ½ teaspoon garlic powder
- Salt and freshly ground black pepper to taste

Directions:

1. Combine the barley and 1½ cups water in a 1-quart 8½ × 8½ × 4-inch ovenproof baking dish. Cover with aluminum foil.

2. BAKE, covered, for 50 minutes, or until almost cooked, testing the grains after 30 minutes for softness.

3. Add the oil and seasonings and fluff with a fork to combine. Cover and let the barley sit for 10 minutes to finish cooking and absorb the flavors of the seasonings. Fluff once more before serving.

Maple Bacon

Servings: 6
Cooking Time: 16 Minutes

Ingredients:

- 12 slices bacon
- ½ cup packed dark brown sugar
- 2 tablespoons maple syrup
- 1 teaspoon Dijon mustard
- 2 tablespoons red or white wine

Directions:

1. Preheat the toaster oven to 350°F. Line a 12 x 12-inch baking pan with aluminum foil.

2. Place 6 bacon strips on the prepared pan, leaving space between the strips. Bake for 10 minutes or until the bacon is almost crisp. Carefully drain the bacon and return it to the pan.

3. Combine the brown sugar, maple syrup, mustard, and wine in a small bowl. Blend until smooth. Brush the glaze over the bacon. Bake for 8 minutes. Turn the bacon and brush with the glaze. Continue to bake for an additional 6 to 8 minutes, or until golden brown.

4. Repeat with the remaining bacon strips.

Sage, Chicken + Mushroom Pasta Casserole

Servings: 6
Cooking Time: 35 Minutes

Ingredients:

- Nonstick cooking spray
- 8 ounces bow-tie pasta, uncooked
- 4 tablespoons unsalted butter
- 8 ounces button or white mushrooms, sliced
- 3 tablespoons all-purpose flour
- Kosher salt and freshly ground black pepper
- 2 cups whole milk
- ½ cup dry white wine
- 2 tablespoons minced fresh sage
- 1 ½ cups chopped cooked chicken
- 1 cup shredded fontina, Monterey Jack, or Swiss cheese
- ½ cup shredded Parmesan cheese

Directions:

1. Preheat the toaster oven to 350°F. Spray a 2-quart baking pan with nonstick cooking spray.

2. Cook the pasta according to the package directions; drain and set aside.

3. Melt the butter in a large skillet over medium-high heat. Add the mushrooms and cook, stirring frequently, until the liquid has evaporated, 7 to 10 minutes. Blend in the flour and cook, stirring constantly, for 1 minute. Season with salt and pepper. Gradually stir in the milk and wine. Cook, stirring constantly, until the mixture bubbles and begins to thicken. Remove from the heat. Stir in the sage, cooked pasta, chicken, and fontina. Season with salt and pepper.

4. Spoon into the prepared pan. Cover and bake for 25 to 30 minutes. Uncover, sprinkle with the

Parmesan, and bake for an additional 5 minutes or until the cheese is melted.

5. Remove from the oven and let stand for 5 to 10 minutes before serving.

Sheet Pan Loaded Nachos

Servings: 4
Cooking Time: 13 Minutes

Ingredients:

- 1 tablespoon canola or vegetable oil
- ½ pound lean ground beef
- ½ cup chopped onion
- 2 cloves garlic, minced
- 1 teaspoon chili powder
- ½ teaspoon ground cumin
- Kosher salt and freshly ground black pepper
- 6 ounces tortilla chips
- ½ cup canned black beans, rinsed and drained
- 1 ½ cups shredded sharp cheddar cheese or Mexican blend cheese
- ½ cup salsa
- Optional toppings: sliced jalapeño peppers, chopped bell peppers, sliced ripe olives, chopped tomatoes, minced fresh cilantro, sour cream, chopped avocado, guacamole, or chopped onion.

Directions:

1. Preheat the toaster oven to 400°F. Line a 12 x 12-inch baking pan with nonstick aluminum foil. (Or if lining the pan with regular foil, spray it with nonstick cooking spray.)

2. Heat the oil in a large skillet over medium-high heat. Add the ground beef and onion and cook, stirring frequently, until the beef is almost done. Add the garlic, chili powder, cumin, season with salt and pepper, and cook, stirring frequently, until the beef is fully cooked; drain.

3. Arrange the tortilla chips in an even layer in the prepared pan. Top with the beef-onion mixture, then top with the beans. Bake, uncovered, for 6 to 8 minutes. Top with the cheese and bake for 5 minutes more, or until the cheese is melted.

4. Drizzle with the salsa. Top as desired with any of the various toppings.

Oven-baked Couscous

Servings: 4
Cooking Time: 10 Minutes

Ingredients:

- 1 10-ounce package couscous
- 2 tablespoons olive oil
- 2 tablespoons canned chickpeas
- 2 tablespoons canned or frozen green peas
- 1 tablespoon chopped fresh parsley
- 3 scallions, chopped
- Salt and pepper to taste

Directions:

1. Preheat the toaster oven to 400° F.

2. Mix together all the ingredients with 2 cups water in a 1-quart 8½ × 8½ × 4-inch ovenproof baking dish. Adjust the seasonings to taste. Cover with aluminum foil.

3. BAKE, covered, for 10 minutes, or until the couscous and vegetables are tender. Adjust the seasonings to taste and fluff with a fork before serving.

Chicken Gumbo

Servings: 4
Cooking Time: 40 Minutes

Ingredients:

- 2 skinless, boneless chicken breast halves, cut into 1-inch cubes

- ½ cup dry red wine
- 1 small onion, finely chopped
- 1 celery stalk, finely chopped
- 2 plum tomatoes, chopped
- 3 1 bell pepper, chopped
- 1 tablespoon minced fresh garlic
- 2 okra pods, stemmed, seeded, and finely chopped 1 bay leaf
- ½ teaspoon hot sauce
- ½ teaspoon dried thyme
- Salt and freshly ground black pepper to taste

Directions:

1. Preheat the toaster oven to 400° F.
2. Combine all the ingredients in a 1-quart 8½ × 8½ × 4-inch ovenproof baking dish. Adjust the seasonings to taste. Cover with aluminum foil.
3. BAKE, covered, for 40 minutes, or until the onion, pepper, and celery are tender. Discard the bay leaf before serving.

Pea Soup

Servings: 6
Cooking Time: 55 Minutes

Ingredients:

- 1 cup dried split peas, ground in a blender to a powderlike consistency
- 3 strips lean turkey bacon, uncooked and chopped
- ¼ cup grated carrots
- ¼ cup grated celery
- 2 tablespoons grated onion
- ½ teaspoon garlic powder
- Salt and freshly ground black pepper to taste
- Garnish:
- 2 tablespoons chopped fresh chives

Directions:

1. Preheat the toaster oven to 400° F.

2. Combine all the ingredients in a 1-quart 8½ × 8½ × 4-inch ovenproof baking dish, mixing well. Adjust the seasonings.

3. BAKE, covered, for 35 minutes. Remove from the oven and stir.

4. BAKE, covered, for another 20 minutes, or until the soup is thickened. Ladle the soup into individual soup bowls and garnish each with chopped fresh chives.

Crunchy Baked Chicken Tenders

Servings: 3-4
Cooking Time: 18 Minutes

Ingredients:

- 2/3 cup seasoned panko breadcrumbs
- 2/3 cup cheese crackers, crushed
- 2 teaspoons melted butter
- 2 large eggs, beaten
- Salt and pepper
- 1 1/2 pounds chicken tenders
- Barbecue sauce

Directions:

1. Preheat the toaster oven to 450°F. Spray the toaster oven baking pan with nonstick cooking spray.

2. In medium bowl, combine breadcrumbs, cheese cracker crumbs and butter.

3. In another medium bowl, mix eggs, salt and pepper.

4. Dip chicken tenders in eggs and dredge in breadcrumb mixture.

5. Place on pan.

6. Bake for 15 to 18 minutes, turning once. Serve with barbecue sauce for dipping.

Chicken Thighs With Roasted Rosemary Root Vegetables

Servings: 2
Cooking Time: 70 Minutes

Ingredients:

- 2 sprigs fresh rosemary
- 1 small turnip, peeled and cut into 1 1/2-inch cubes
- 1 parsnip, peeled and cut into 1/2-inch slices
- 1 small onion, quartered
- 1 large sweet potato, peeled and cut into 1-inch cubes
- 2 cloves garlic, peeled
- 2 tablespoons olive oil
- 1 teaspoon salt, divided
- 1/2 teaspoon coarse pepper, divided
- 1/2 teaspoon rotisserie chicken seasoning
- 4 chicken thighs with bone and skin

Directions:

1. Place rack on bottom position of toaster oven. Preheat the toaster oven to 425°F.
2. Spray the toaster oven baking pan with nonstick cooking spray. Place rosemary sprigs on pan.
3. In a large bowl, mix turnip. parsnip, onion, sweet potato, garlic, oil, 1/2 teaspoon salt and 1/4 teaspoon pepper until vegetables are coated with oil. Add to baking pan.
4. Bake 30 minutes. Stir vegetables.
5. Sprinkle remaining salt, pepper and rotisserie chicken seasoning over chicken pieces.
6. Place chicken on top of vegetables in pan. Continue baking for an additional 35 to 40 minutes or until chicken reaches 165°F when tested with a meat thermometer and vegetables are roasted.

Lima Bean And Artichoke Casserole

Servings: 4
Cooking Time: 40 Minutes

Ingredients:

- 1 15-ounce can lima beans, drained
- 1 6-ounce jar artichokes, marinated in olive oil (include the oil)
- ½ cup dry white wine
- 1 small onion, thinly sliced
- 2 medium carrots, thinly sliced
- 1 5-ounce can roasted peppers, drained and chopped
- ¼ teaspoon paprika
- ½ teaspoon ground cumin
- 1 teaspoon curry powder
- Salt and freshly ground black pepper to taste

Directions:

1. Preheat the toaster oven to 350° F.
2. Combine all the ingredients in a 1-quart 8½ × 8½ × 4-inch ovenproof baking dish, blending well Adjust the seasonings to taste. Cover with aluminum foil.
3. BAKE, covered, for 40 minutes, or until the carrots and onion are tender.

Salad Lentils

Servings: 4
Cooking Time: 35 Minutes

Ingredients:

- ¼ cup lentils
- 1 tablespoon olive oil
- Salad ingredients:
- 1 celery stalk, trimmed and Chopped
- 1 plum tomato, chopped
- 1 cucumber, peeled, seeded, and chopped

- 1½ cups spinach leaves, pulled into small pieces
- 1 tablespoon balsamic vinegar
- 1 tablespoon olive oil
- ½ teaspoon dried oregano
- 1 tablespoon chopped scallions
- 2 tablespoons sliced pitted black olives
- 1 teaspoon minced roasted garlic

Directions:

1. Preheat the toaster oven to 400° F.
2. Combine the lentils, ¼ cups water, and olive oil in a 1-quart 8½ × 8½ × 4-inch ovenproof baking dish. Cover with aluminum foil.
3. BAKE, covered, for 35 minutes, or until the lentils are tender. When cool, combine with all the salad ingredients in a serving bowl and toss well. Adjust the seasonings, chill, and serve.

Broiled Chipotle Tilapia With Avocado Sauce

Servings: 2
Cooking Time: 10 Minutes

Ingredients:

- 1 small avocado, halved, pitted and peeled
- 3 tablespoons sour cream
- 1 teaspoon lime juice
- 2 1/2 teaspoons chipotle and roasted garlic seasoning, divided
- 1 tablespoon mayonnaise
- 1/2 pound tilapia fillets
- Chopped cilantro

Directions:

1. Using a chopper or small food processor, blend avocado, sour cream, lime juice and 1 1/2 teaspoons seasoning until smooth. Cover and refrigerate.
2. Spray toaster oven baking pan with nonstick cooking spray.

3. in small bowl, mix mayonnaise and remaining 1 teaspoon seasoning.
4. Brush mayonnaise mixture on both sides of tilapia fillets.
5. Place coated fish in pan.
6. Set toaster oven to BROIL. Broil fish for 10 minutes or until fish flakes with a fork.
7. Serve with avocado sauce and garnish with lime slices and cilantro, if desired.

Homemade Pizza Sauce

Servings: 1
Cooking Time: 20 Minutes

Ingredients:

- 1 9-inch ready-made pizza crust or 1 homemade pizza crust
- 2 plum tomatoes, chopped
- 1 tablespoon olive oil
- 3 garlic cloves, peeled and chopped ¼ cup chopped onion
- 2 tablespoons tomato paste
- 2 tablespoons dry red wine
- 1 tablespoon chopped fresh basil or 1 teaspoon dried basil
- 1 tablespoon chopped fresh oregano or 1 teaspoon dried oregano
- 1 bay leaf
- Salt and freshly ground black pepper to taste

Directions:

1. Combine all ingredients in an 8½ × 8½ × 2-inch square baking (cake) pan. Adjust the seasonings to taste.
2. BROIL for 20 minutes, or until the onions and tomatoes are tender. Remove the bay leaf and cool before spreading on the pizza crust. Bake the pizza according to instructions on the ready-made crust package or in the homemade pizza crust recipe.

Rosemary Lentils

Servings: 2

Cooking Time: 35 Minutes

Ingredients:

- ¼ cup lentils
- 1 tablespoon mashed Roasted Garlic
- 1 rosemary sprig
- 1 bay leaf
- Salt and freshly ground black pepper
- 2 tablespoons low-fat buttermilk
- 2 tablespoons tomato sauce

Directions:

1. Preheat the toaster oven to 400° F.

2. Combine the lentils, 1¼ cups water, garlic, rosemary sprig, and bay leaf in a 1-quart 8½ × 8½ × 4-inch ovenproof baking dish, stirring to blend well. Add the salt and pepper to taste. Cover with aluminum foil.

3. BAKE, covered, for 35 minutes, or until the lentils are tender. Remove the rosemary sprig and bay leaf and stir in the buttermilk and tomato sauce. Serve immediately.

Kasha Loaf

Servings: 4

Cooking Time: 30 Minutes

Ingredients:

- 1 cup whole grain kasha
- 2 cups tomato sauce or 3 2 8-ounce cans tomato sauce (add a small amount of water to make 4 2 cups)
- 3 tablespoons minced onion or scallions
- 1 tablespoon minced garlic
- 1 cup multigrain bread crumbs
- 1 egg
- 1 teaspoon paprika
- 1 teaspoon chili powder

- 1 teaspoon sesame oil

Directions:

1. Preheat the toaster oven to 400° F.

2. Combine all the ingredients in a bowl and transfer to an oiled or nonstick regular-size 4½ × 8½ × 2/4-inch loaf pan.

3. BAKE, uncovered, for 30 minutes, or until lightly browned.

Italian Baked Stuffed Tomatoes

Servings: 4

Cooking Time: 30 Minutes

Ingredients:

- 4 large tomatoes
- 1 cup shredded chicken
- 1 1/2 cup shredded mozzarella, divided
- 1 1/2 cup cooked rice
- 2 tablespoon minced onion
- 1/4 cup grated parmesan cheese
- 1 tablespoon dried Italian seasoning
- salt
- pepper
- Basil

Directions:

1. Preheat the toaster oven to 350°F. Spray toaster oven pan with nonstick cooking spray.

2. Cut the top off each tomato and scoop centers out. Place bottoms on prepared pan. Chop 3 tomatoes (about 1 1/2 cup, chopped) and add to large bowl.

3. Add shredded chicken, 1 cup shredded mozzarella cheese, rice, onion, Parmesan cheese, Italian seasoning, salt and pepper to large bowl and stir until blended. Divide between tomatoes, about 1 cup per tomato. Top with remaining mozzarella and tomato top.

4. Bake 25 to 30 minutes until cheese is melted and mixture is heated through.

5. Garnish with basil before serving.

Individual Baked Eggplant Parmesan

Servings: 5
Cooking Time: 55 Minutes

Ingredients:

* 1 medium eggplant, cut into 1/2-inch thick slices
* 1 1/2 teaspoons salt
* 1 cup Slow Cooker Marinara Sauce
* 1 package (8 oz.) fresh mozzarella, cut into 8 slices, divided
* 1 package (0.75 oz.) fresh basil, leaves only, divided
* 1/4 cup grated Parmesan cheese, divided

Directions:

1. Sprinkle eggplant with salt and place in a colander to drain for 1 hour.
2. Preheat the toaster oven to 375°F. Spray baking pan and 5 (4-inch) ramekins with nonstick cooking spray.
3. Rinse eggplant thoroughly with water to remove salt. Press each slice between paper towels to remove extra water and salt. Place on papertowels to dry. Arrange a single layer of eggplant slices in baking pan.
4. Bake 25 to 30 minutes or until eggplant is tender. Remove slices to cooking rack. Repeat baking remaining eggplant. Reduce oven temperature to 350°F.
5. In each ramekin, layer 1 slice eggplant, 1 tablespoon sauce, 1 slice mozzarella, 1 basil leaf, 1 additional tablespoon sauce and sprinkle with Parmesan cheese. Repeat layers ending with a sprinkle of Parmesan cheese.
6. Bake 20 to 25 minutes or until cheese is melted and eggplant layers are heated through.

Cornucopia Casserole

Servings: 4
Cooking Time: 45 Minutes

Ingredients:

* 1 celery stalk, chopped
* 2 tablespoons chopped Vidalia onion
* 3 ½ bell pepper, chopped
* 1 carrot, peeled and chopped
* 1 small zucchini, chopped
* ½ cup green beans, cut into 1-inch Pieces
* ½ cup frozen peas ½ cup frozen corn
* ½ cup frozen broccoli florets
* ½ cup frozen cauliflower florets
* 2 tablespoons vegetable oil
* 1 teaspoon ground cumin
* 1 teaspoon garlic powder
* ½ teaspoon paprika
* Salt and freshly ground black pepper to taste
* ½ cup finely chopped pecans
* 3 tablespoons grated Parmesan cheese

Directions:

1. Preheat the toaster oven to 400° F.
2. Combine all the ingredients, except the pecans and Parmesan cheese, in a 1-quart 8½ × 8½ × 4-inch ovenproof baking dish and adjust the seasonings to taste. Cover with aluminum foil.
3. BAKE, covered, for 35 minutes, or until the vegetables are tender. Uncover, stir to distribute the liquid, and adjust the seasonings again. Sprinkle the top with the pecans and Parmesan cheese.
4. BROIL for 10 minutes, or until the pecans are lightly browned.

Tomato Bisque

Servings: 4
Cooking Time: 25 Minutes

Ingredients:

- 1 8-ounce can tomato sauce
- 1 7-ounce jar diced pimientos, drained
- 1 tablespoon finely chopped onion
- 2 cups low-fat buttermilk
- 1 cup fat-free half-and-half
- 1 tablespoon low-fat cream cheese
- 1 teaspoon garlic powder
- ½ teaspoon paprika
- ½ teaspoon ground bay leaf
- 1 teaspoon hot sauce (optional)
- Salt and white pepper to taste
- 2 tablespoons minced fresh basil leaves

Directions:

1. Preheat the toaster oven to 350° F.
2. Process all the ingredients except the basil in a blender or food processor until smooth. Pour into a 1-quart 8½ × 8½ × 4-inch ovenproof baking dish. Adjust the seasonings to taste.
3. BAKE, covered, for 25 minutes. Ladle into small soup bowls and garnish each with fresh basil leaves before serving.

French Onion Soup

Servings: 4
Cooking Time: 46 Minutes

Ingredients:

- 1 cup finely chopped onions
- 1 teaspoon toasted sesame oil
- 1 tablespoon vegetable oil
- 2 ½ cup dry white wine
- 3 teaspoons soy sauce
- ½ teaspoon garlic powder
- Freshly ground black pepper to taste
- 4 French bread rounds, sliced 1 inch thick
- 4 tablespoons grated Parmesan cheese
- 1 tablespoon chopped fresh parsley

Directions:

1. Place the onions, sesame oil, and vegetable oil in an 8½ × 8½ × 2-inch square baking (cake) pan.
2. BROIL for 10 minutes, stirring every 3 minutes until the onions are tender. Remove from the oven and transfer to a 1-quart 8½ × 8½ × 4-inch ovenproof baking dish. Add 2 cups water, the wine, and the soy sauce. Add the garlic powder and pepper and adjust the seasonings.
3. BAKE, covered, at 400° F. for 30 minutes. Remove from the oven, uncover, and add the 4 bread rounds, letting them float on top of the soup. Sprinkle each with 1 tablespoon Parmesan cheese.
4. BROIL, uncovered, for 6 minutes, or until the cheese is lightly browned. With tongs, transfer the bread rounds to 4 individual soup bowls. Ladle the soup on top of the bread rounds. Garnish with the parsley and serve immediately.

SNACKS APPETIZERS AND SIDES

Eggs In Avocado Halves

Servings: 3
Cooking Time: 23 Minutes

Ingredients:
- 3 Hass avocados, halved and pitted but not peeled
- 6 Medium eggs
- Vegetable oil spray
- 3 tablespoons Heavy or light cream (not fat-free cream)
- To taste Table salt
- To taste Ground black pepper

Directions:
1. Preheat the toaster oven to 350°F .
2. Slice a small amount off the (skin) side of each avocado half so it can sit stable, without rocking. Lightly coat the skin of the avocado half (the side that will now sit stable) with vegetable oil spray.
3. Arrange the avocado halves open side up on a cutting board, then crack an egg into the indentation in each where the pit had been. If any white overflows the avocado half, wipe that bit of white off the cut edge of the avocado before proceeding.
4. Remove the pan (or its attachment) from the machine and set the filled avocado halves in it in one layer. Return it to the machine without pushing it in. Drizzle each avocado half with about 1½ teaspoons cream, a little salt, and a little ground black pepper.
5. Air-fry undisturbed for 10 minutes for a soft-set yolk, or air-fry for 13 minutes for more-set eggs.

6. Use a nonstick-safe spatula and a flatware fork for balance to transfer the avocado halves to serving plates. Cool a minute or two before serving.

Mozzarella-stuffed Arancini

Servings: 14
Cooking Time: 20 Minutes

Ingredients:
- Pie Crust
- 3½ cups low sodium chicken stock
- 4 tablespoons unsalted butter, divided
- 1 medium onion, finely chopped
- 2 garlic cloves, minced
- 1 cup arborio rice
- 1½ teaspoons kosher salt, plus more to taste
- ½ cup dry white wine
- 2 ounces finely grated Parmesan
- ¼ cup heavy cream
- 1 teaspoon freshly ground black pepper, plus more to taste
- 3 ounces low-moisture mozzarella, cut into ⅓-inch pieces
- 1½ cups panko breadcrumbs
- 2 tablespoons melted salted butter
- ½ cup all-purpose flour 2 large eggs, beaten Cooking spray
- Marinara sauce, for serving

Directions:
1. Simmer chicken stock in a pot, then keep warm on low heat.
2. Heat 2 tablespoons of unsalted butter in a medium saucepan over medium heat.
3. Add onions to the saucepan and cook for 5 minutes or until softened.

4. Add garlic and cook for 1 minute or until softened.

5. Add rice and 1½ teaspoons of kosher salt to the saucepan.

6. Cook the rice for 3 minutes or until the edges turn translucent.

7. Pour in the wine, stir, and cook for 3 minutes or until the wine is all evaporated and the rice looks dry.

8. Ladle in 1 cup of the warm chicken stock and bring to a simmer. Stirring often, cook the rice for 5 minutes or until liquid is absorbed. Repeat this process with another cup of chicken stock.

9. Add the remaining 1½ cups of chicken stock and cook, stirring often, for 10 minutes or until the rice is cooked through but toothsome and the liquid is mostly absorbed.

10. Remove the risotto from the heat and mix in Parmesan, heavy cream, black pepper, and the remaining two tablespoons of unsalted butter.

11. Season the risotto to taste with salt and black pepper.

12. Spread risotto in an even layer on a parchment-lined baking sheet and cover with plastic wrap.

13. Place the risotto in the fridge and chill for 4 hours.

14. Seperate the chilled risotto into 14 even pieces and form them into round patties about 2½ inches in diameter.

15. Place a piece of mozzarella in the center of a patty, pinch and shape the risotto so it completely encases the cheese, then roll into a ball. Repeat with each risotto patty.

16. Place the balls onto the baking sheet lined with fresh parchment paper, cover with plastic wrap, and place in the freezer for 15 minutes.

17. Place the panko breadcrumbs into a food processor and pulse until finely ground, then place into a bowl.

18. Mix the panko breadcrumbs with the melted salted butter until well combined.

19. Remove the risotto balls from the freezer and dredge in flour, dip in beaten eggs, then cover with breadcrumbs. Repeat this process with the rest of the balls. Set aside.

20. Preheat the toaster oven to 400°F.

21. Place the balls into the fry basket, spray them liberally with cooking spray, then insert the basket at mid position in the preheated oven.

22. Select the Air Fry function, adjust time to 20 minutes, and press Start/Pause.

23. Remove the arancini from the oven and serve with marinara sauce.

Thick-crust Pepperoni Pizza

Servings: 2
Cooking Time: 10 Minutes

Ingredients:

• 10 ounces Purchased fresh pizza dough (not a prebaked crust)

• Olive oil spray

• ¼ cup Purchased pizza sauce

• 10 slices Sliced pepperoni

• ⅓ cup Purchased shredded Italian 3- or 4-cheese blend

Directions:

1. Preheat the toaster oven to 400°F.

2. Generously coat the inside of a 6-inch round cake pan for a small air fryer oven, a 7-inch round cake pan for a medium air fryer oven, or an 8-inch round cake pan for a large model with olive oil spray.

3. Set the dough in the pan and press it to fill the bottom in an even, thick layer. Spread the sauce over the dough, then top with the pepperoni and cheese.

4. When the machine is at temperature, set the pan in the air fryer oven and air-fry undisturbed for 10 minutes, or until puffed, brown, and bubbling.

5. Use kitchen tongs to transfer the cake pan to a wire rack. Cool for only a minute or so. Use a spatula to loosen the pizza from the pan and lift it out and onto the rack. Continue cooling for a few minutes before cutting into wedges to serve.

Simple Holiday Stuffing

Servings: 4
Cooking Time: 120 Minutes

Ingredients:

• 12 ounces hearty white sandwich bread, cut into ½-inch pieces (8 cups)
• 1 onion, chopped fine
• 1 celery rib, chopped fine
• 1 tablespoon unsalted butter, plus 5 tablespoons, melted
• 1 tablespoon minced fresh thyme or 1 teaspoon dried
• 2 teaspoons minced fresh sage or ½ teaspoon dried
• ¾ teaspoon table salt
• ¼ teaspoon pepper
• 1¼ cups chicken broth

Directions:

1. Adjust toaster oven rack to middle position and preheat the toaster oven to 300 degrees. Spread bread into even layer on small rimmed baking sheet and bake until light golden brown, 35 to 45 minutes, tossing halfway through baking. Let bread cool completely on sheet.

2. Increase oven temperature to 375 degrees. Microwave onion, celery, 1 tablespoon butter, thyme, sage, salt, and pepper in covered large bowl, stirring occasionally, until vegetables are softened, 2 to 4 minutes.

3. Stir in broth, then add bread and toss to combine. Let mixture sit for 10 minutes, then toss mixture again until broth is fully absorbed. Transfer bread mixture to 8-inch square baking dish or pan and distribute evenly but do not pack down. (Stuffing can be covered and refrigerated for up to 24 hours; increase covered baking time to 15 minutes.)

4. Drizzle melted butter evenly over top of stuffing. Cover dish tightly with aluminum foil and bake for 10 minutes. Uncover and continue to bake until top is golden brown and crisp, 15 to 25 minutes. Transfer dish to wire rack and let cool for 10 minutes. Serve.

Sweet Plantain Chips

Servings: 4
Cooking Time: 11 Minutes

Ingredients:

• 2 Very ripe plantain(s), peeled and sliced into 1-inch pieces
• Vegetable oil spray
• 3 tablespoons Maple syrup
• For garnishing Coarse sea salt or kosher salt

Directions:

1. Pour about ½ cup water into the bottom of your air fryer oven or into a metal tray on a lower rack in some models. Preheat the toaster oven to 400°F.

2. Put the plantain pieces in a bowl, coat them with vegetable oil spray, and toss gently, spraying at least one more time and tossing repeatedly, until the pieces are well coated.

3. When the machine is at temperature, arrange the plantain pieces in the air fryer oven in one layer. Air-fry undisturbed for 5 minutes.

4. Remove the pan from the machine and spray the back of a metal spatula with vegetable oil spray. Use the spatula to press down on the plantain pieces, spraying it again as needed, to flatten the pieces to about half their original height. Brush the plantain pieces with maple syrup, then return the pan to the machine and continue air-frying undisturbed for 6 minutes, or until the plantain pieces are soft and caramelized.

5. Use kitchen tongs to transfer the pieces to a serving platter. Sprinkle the pieces with salt and cool for a couple of minutes before serving. Or cool to room temperature before serving, about 1 hour.

Roasted Brussels Sprouts Au Gratin

Servings: 6
Cooking Time: 36 Minutes

Ingredients:

- 1 pound fresh Brussels sprouts, trimmed and halved
- 2 tablespoons olive oil
- Kosher salt and freshly ground black pepper
- Nonstick cooking spray
- 2 slices bacon, cooked until crisp and crumbled
- 3 tablespoons unsalted butter
- 2 tablespoons all-purpose flour
- 1 cup whole milk
- 1 cup shredded Gruyère or Swiss cheese
- ½ teaspoon dried thyme leaves
- ¼ cup panko bread crumbs
- ¼ cup shredded Parmesan cheese

Directions:

1. Preheat the toaster oven to 450°F.

2. Toss the Brussels sprouts with the olive oil in a large bowl. Season with salt and pepper. Arrange the Brussels sprouts in a single layer in a 12 x 12-inch baking pan. Bake uncovered for 10 minutes. Stir and bake for an additional 8 to 10 minutes, or until the edges are beginning to char and the Brussels sprouts are just tender. Remove from the oven.

3. Reduce the toaster oven to 375°F. Spray a 1 ½-quart casserole dish or an 8 x 8-inch square baking pan with nonstick cooking spray. Place the Brussels sprouts in the casserole dish. Sprinkle with the crisp bacon.

4. Melt 2 tablespoons of the butter in a small saucepan over medium heat. Stir in the flour, blending until smooth and cook, stirring constantly, for 1 minute. Gradually add the milk and cook, stirring constantly, until the mixture is bubbly and thickened. Season with salt and pepper. Stir in the cheese and thyme and cook, stirring until melted. Pour the sauce over the Brussels sprouts.

5. Melt the remaining tablespoon of butter. Stir in the panko bread crumbs and Parmesan cheese. Sprinkle the bread crumb mixture over the casserole. Bake, uncovered, for 15 minutes or until golden brown and the edges are bubbling.

Cheese Straws

Servings: 8
Cooking Time: 7 Minutes

Ingredients:

- For dusting All-purpose flour
- Two quarters of one thawed sheet (that is, a half of the sheet cut into two even pieces; wrap and refreeze the remainder) A 17.25-ounce box frozen puff pastry
- 1 Large egg(s)
- 2 tablespoons Water
- ¼ cup (about ¾ ounce) Finely grated Parmesan cheese
- up to 1 teaspoon Ground black pepper

Directions:

1. Preheat the toaster oven to 400°F.
2. Dust a clean, dry work surface with flour. Set one of the pieces of puff pastry on top, dust the pastry lightly with flour, and roll with a rolling pin to a 6-inch square.
3. Whisk the egg(s) and water in a small or medium bowl until uniform. Brush the pastry square(s) generously with this mixture. Sprinkle each square with 2 tablespoons grated cheese and up to ½ teaspoon ground black pepper.
4. Cut each square into 4 even strips. Grasp each end of 1 strip with clean, dry hands; twist it into a cheese straw. Place the twisted straws on a baking sheet.
5. Lay as many straws as will fit in the air-fryer oven—as a general rule, 4 of them in a small machine, 5 in a medium model, or 6 in a large. There should be space for air to circulate around the straws. Set the baking sheet with any remaining straws in the fridge.
6. Air-fry undisturbed for 7 minutes, or until puffed and crisp. Use tongs to transfer the cheese straws to a wire rack, then make subsequent batches in the same way (keeping the baking sheet with the remaining straws in the fridge as each batch cooks). Serve warm.

Spanakopita Spinach, Feta And Pine Nut Phyllo Bites

Servings: 8
Cooking Time: 10 Minutes

Ingredients:

- ½ (10-ounce) package frozen spinach, thawed and squeezed dry (about 1 cup)
- ¾ cup crumbled feta cheese
- ¼ cup grated Parmesan cheese
- ¼ cup pine nuts, toasted
- ⅛ teaspoon ground nutmeg
- 1 egg, lightly beaten
- ½ teaspoon salt
- freshly ground black pepper
- 6 sheets phyllo dough
- ½ cup butter, melted

Directions:

1. Combine the spinach, cheeses, pine nuts, nutmeg and egg in a bowl. Season with salt and freshly ground black pepper.
2. While building the phyllo triangles, always keep the dough sheets you are not working with covered with plastic wrap and a damp clean kitchen towel. Remove one sheet of the phyllo and place it on a flat surface. Brush the phyllo sheet with melted butter and then layer another sheet of phyllo on top. Brush the second sheet of phyllo with butter. Cut the layered phyllo sheets into 6 strips, about 2½- to 3-inches wide.
3. Place a heaping tablespoon of the spinach filling at the end of each strip of dough. Fold the bottom right corner of the strip over the filling

towards the left edge of the strip to make a triangle. Continue to fold the phyllo dough around the spinach as you would fold a flag, making triangle after triangle. Brush the outside of the phyllo triangle with more melted butter and set it aside until you've finished the 6 strips of dough, making 6 triangles.

4. Preheat the toaster oven to 350°F.

5. Transfer the first six phyllo triangles to the air fryer oven and air-fry for 5 minutes. Turn the triangles over and air-fry for another 5 minutes.

6. While the first batch of triangles is air-frying, build another set of triangles and air-fry in the same manner. You should do three batches total. These can be warmed in the air fryer oven for a minute or two just before serving if you like.

Cinnamon Pita Chips

Servings: 4
Cooking Time: 6 Minutes

Ingredients:

- 2 tablespoons sugar
- 2 teaspoons cinnamon
- 2 whole 6-inch pitas, whole grain or white
- oil for misting or cooking spray

Directions:

1. Mix sugar and cinnamon together.

2. Cut each pita in half and each half into 4 wedges. Break apart each wedge at the fold.

3. Mist one side of pita wedges with oil or cooking spray. Sprinkle them all with half of the cinnamon sugar.

4. Turn the wedges over, mist the other side with oil or cooking spray, and sprinkle with the remaining cinnamon sugar.

5. Place pita wedges in air fryer oven and air-fry at 330°F for 2 minutes.

6. Cook 2 more minutes. If needed cook 2 more minutes, until crisp. Watch carefully because at this point they will cook very quickly.

Spinach And Artichoke Dip

Servings: 6
Cooking Time: 45 Minutes

Ingredients:

- 6 ounces cream cheese, softened
- ½ cup mayonnaise
- 2 tablespoons water
- 1 tablespoon lemon juice
- 3 garlic cloves, minced
- ¼ teaspoon table salt
- ¼ teaspoon pepper
- 3 cups jarred whole baby artichokes packed in water, rinsed, patted dry, and chopped
- 10 ounces frozen spinach, thawed and squeezed dry
- 2 tablespoons minced fresh chives

Directions:

1. Adjust toaster oven rack to middle position and preheat the toaster oven to 400 degrees. Whisk cream cheese, mayonnaise, water, lemon juice, garlic, salt, and pepper in large bowl until well combined. Gently fold in artichokes and spinach. Transfer mixture to 2-quart baking dish and smooth top with rubber spatula.

2. Bake until spotty golden brown and bubbling around edges, 20 to 25 minutes. Transfer dish to wire rack and let cool for 10 minutes. Sprinkle with chives and serve.

Roasted Fennel With Wine + Parmesan

Servings: 3
Cooking Time: 26 Minutes

Ingredients:

- 3 medium fennel bulbs, trimmed, cored, and cut horizontally into ⅓-inch-thick slices, reserving 2 teaspoons fronds (leaves)
- 2 ½ tablespoons olive oil, plus more for greasing
- Kosher salt and freshly ground black pepper
- 2 tablespoons dry white wine
- 3 tablespoons shredded Parmesan cheese

Directions:

1. Preheat the toaster oven to 425 ºF. Lightly oil a 12 x 12-inch baking pan.
2. Arrange the fennel in a single layer on the prepared pan. Drizzle the olive oil evenly over and season with salt and pepper. Stir to blend well and arrange in a single layer. Roast for 12 minutes. Stir and roast for an additional 10 to 12 minutes, or until the fennel is brown and crisp around the edges and the largest piece is tender when pierced with the tip of a knife.
3. Carefully remove the pan from the oven. Drizzle the wine over the cooked fennel and sprinkle with the Parmesan cheese. Return to the oven and bake for an additional 2 minutes or until the cheese is melted. Sprinkle with the reserved fronds before serving warm.

Baked Asparagus Fries

Servings: 2-3
Cooking Time: 14 Minutes

Ingredients:

- 1 1/2 cups mayonnaise
- 3/4 cup grated Parmesan cheese
- 2 cloves garlic, minced
- 1 tablespoon dried parsley
- 1 tablespoon Italian seasoning
- 1 teaspoon salt
- 1/2 teaspoon coarse black pepper
- 1/2 pound thick asparagus, trimmed
- 1 cup panko crumbs

Directions:

1. Heat the oven to 425ºF.
2. In a small bowl, combine mayonnaise, Parmesan cheese, garlic, parsley, Italian seasoning, salt and black pepper.
3. Brush asparagus with 3 tablespoons mayonnaise mixture and roll in crumbs. Place asparagus on the baking pan.
4. Bake 12 to 14 minutes or until lightly browned and asparagus are cooked.
5. Serve asparagus with the remaining mayonnaise mixture.

Cherry Chipotle Bbq Chicken Wings

Servings: 2
Cooking Time: 12 Minutes

Ingredients:

- 1 teaspoon smoked paprika
- ½ teaspoon dry mustard powder
- 1 teaspoon dried oregano
- 1 teaspoon dried thyme
- ½ teaspoon chili powder
- 1 teaspoon salt
- 2 pounds chicken wings
- vegetable oil or spray
- salt and freshly ground black pepper
- 1 to 2 tablespoons chopped chipotle peppers in adobo sauce

- ⅓ cup cherry preserves ¼ cup tomato ketchup

Directions:

1. Combine the first six ingredients in a large bowl. Prepare the chicken wings by cutting off the wing tips and discarding (or freezing for chicken stock). Divide the drumettes from the win-gettes by cutting through the joint. Place the chicken wing pieces in the bowl with the spice mix. Toss or shake well to coat.

2. Preheat the toaster oven to 400°F.

3. Spray the wings lightly with the vegetable oil and air-fry the wings in two batches for 10 minutes per batch. When both batches are done, toss all the wings back into the air fryer oven for another 2 minutes to heat through and finish cooking.

4. While the wings are air-frying, combine the chopped chipotle peppers, cherry preserves and ketchup in a bowl.

5. Remove the wings from the air fryer oven, toss them in the cherry chipotle BBQ sauce and serve with napkins!

Roasted Green Beans With Goat Cheese And Hazelnuts

Servings: 2
Cooking Time: 45 Minutes

Ingredients:

- 12 ounces green beans, trimmed
- 3 tablespoons extra-virgin olive oil, divided
- ¼ teaspoon sugar
- ¼ teaspoon plus ⅛ teaspoon table salt, divided
- ¼ teaspoon plus ⅛ teaspoon pepper, divided
- 1 garlic clove, minced
- ½ teaspoon grated orange zest plus 1 teaspoon juice
- 1 teaspoon lemon juice

- ½ teaspoon Dijon mustard
- 1 tablespoon minced fresh chives
- 1 ounce goat cheese, crumbled (¼ cup)
- 2 tablespoons chopped toasted hazelnuts

Directions:

1. Adjust toaster oven rack to lowest position and preheat the toaster oven to 450 degrees. Toss green beans, 1 tablespoon oil, sugar, ¼ teaspoon salt, and ¼ teaspoon pepper together in bowl, then spread into even layer on small rimmed baking sheet.

2. Cover sheet tightly with aluminum foil and roast for 12 minutes. Remove foil and continue to roast until green beans are spotty brown, 10 to 15 minutes.

3. Meanwhile, combine garlic, orange zest, and remaining 2 tablespoons oil in large bowl and microwave until fragrant, 30 to 60 seconds; let steep for 1 minute. Whisk in orange juice, lemon juice, mustard, remaining ⅛ teaspoon salt, and remaining ⅛ teaspoon pepper. Add green beans and chives and toss to combine. Transfer to serving platter and sprinkle with goat cheese and hazelnuts. Serve.

Fried Apple Wedges

Servings: 4
Cooking Time: 9 Minutes

Ingredients:

- ¼ cup panko breadcrumbs
- ¼ cup pecans
- 1½ teaspoons cinnamon
- 1½ teaspoons brown sugar
- ¼ cup cornstarch
- 1 egg white
- 2 teaspoons water
- 1 medium apple

- oil for misting or cooking spray

Directions:

1. In a food processor, combine panko, pecans, cinnamon, and brown sugar. Process to make small crumbs.
2. Place cornstarch in a plastic bag or bowl with lid. In a shallow dish, beat together the egg white and water until slightly foamy.
3. Preheat the toaster oven to 390°F.
4. Cut apple into small wedges. The thickest edge should be no more than ⅜- to ½-inch thick. Cut away the core, but do not peel.
5. Place apple wedges in cornstarch, reseal bag or bowl, and shake to coat.
6. Dip wedges in egg wash, shake off excess, and roll in crumb mixture. Spray with oil.
7. Place apples in air fryer oven in single layer and air-fry for 5 minutes.Break apart any apples that have stuck together. Mist lightly with oil and cook 4 minutes longer, until crispy.

Cinnamon Apple Chips

Servings: 4
Cooking Time: 480 Minutes

Ingredients:

- 1 apple
- 1 tablespoon lemon juice
- ¼ teaspoon cinnamon

Directions:

1. Slice the apple into ⅛-inch-thick slices, preferably by using a mandoline slicer.
2. Place slices in a bowl of water mixed with the lemon juice to prevent browning. Remove after 2 minutes and dry thoroughly with paper towels.
3. Sprinkle the apple slices with cinnamon and place on the food tray.
4. Insert the food tray at mid position in the preheated oven.
5. Preheat the toaster oven to 130°F.
6. Remove when apple chips are crispy.

Ham And Cheese Palmiers

Servings: 30
Cooking Time: 60 Minutes

Ingredients:

- 1 (9½ by 9-inch) sheet puff pastry, thawed
- 2 tablespoons Dijon mustard
- 2 teaspoons minced fresh thyme
- 2 ounces Parmesan cheese, grated (1 cup)
- 4 ounces thinly sliced deli ham

Directions:

1. Roll puff pastry into 12-inch square on lightly floured counter. Brush evenly with mustard; sprinkle with thyme and Parmesan; pressing gently to adhere, and lay ham evenly over top. Roll up opposite sides of pastry until they meet in middle. Wrap pastry log in plastic wrap and refrigerate until firm, about 1 hour.
2. Adjust toaster oven rack to middle position, select air-fry or convection setting, and preheat the toaster oven to 400 degrees. Line large and small rimmed baking sheets with parchment paper. Using sharp knife, trim ends of log, then slice into ⅓-inch-thick pieces. Space desired number of palmiers at least 1 inch apart on prepared small sheet; space remaining palmiers evenly on prepared large sheet. Re-shape palmiers as needed.
3. Bake small sheet of palmiers until golden brown and crisp, 15 to 25 minutes. Transfer palmiers to wire rack and let cool for 15 minutes before serving. (Palmiers can be held at room temperature for up to 6 hours before serving.)

4. Freeze remaining large sheet of palmiers until firm, about 1 hour. Transfer palmiers to 1-gallon zipper-lock bag and freeze for up to 1 month. Cook frozen palmiers as directed; do not thaw.

Warm And Salty Edamame

Servings: 4
Cooking Time: 10 Minutes

Ingredients:
- 1 pound Unshelled edamame
- Vegetable oil spray
- ¾ teaspoon Coarse sea salt or kosher salt

Directions:
1. Preheat the toaster oven to 400°F.
2. Place the edamame in a large bowl and lightly coat them with vegetable oil spray. Toss well, spray again, and toss until they are evenly coated.
3. When the machine is at temperature, pour the edamame into the air fryer oven and air-fry, tossing the pan quite often to rearrange the edamame, for 7 minutes, or until warm and aromatic. (Air-fry for 10 minutes if the edamame were frozen and not thawed.)
4. Pour the edamame into a bowl and sprinkle the salt on top. Toss well, then set aside for a couple of minutes before serving with an empty bowl on the side for the pods.

Grilled Ham & Muenster Cheese On Raisin Bread

Servings: 1
Cooking Time: 10 Minutes

Ingredients:
- 2 slices raisin bread
- 2 tablespoons butter, softened
- 2 teaspoons honey mustard
- 3 slices thinly sliced honey ham (about 3 ounces)
- 4 slices Muenster cheese (about 3 ounces)
- 2 toothpicks

Directions:
1. Preheat the toaster oven to 370°F.
2. Spread the softened butter on one side of both slices of raisin bread and place the bread, buttered side down on the counter. Spread the honey mustard on the other side of each slice of bread. Layer 2 slices of cheese, the ham and the remaining 2 slices of cheese on one slice of bread and top with the other slice of bread. Remember to leave the buttered side of the bread on the outside.
3. Transfer the sandwich to the air fryer oven and secure the sandwich with toothpicks.
4. Air-fry at 370°F for 5 minutes. Flip the sandwich over, remove the toothpicks and air-fry for another 5 minutes. Cut the sandwich in half and enjoy!!

Crispy Tofu Bites

Servings: 4
Cooking Time: 20 Minutes

Ingredients:
- 1 pound Extra firm unflavored tofu
- Vegetable oil spray

Directions:
1. Wrap the piece of tofu in a triple layer of paper towels. Place it on a wooden cutting board and set a large pot on top of it to press out excess moisture. Set aside for 10 minutes.
2. Preheat the toaster oven to 400°F.
3. Remove the pot and unwrap the tofu. Cut it into 1-inch cubes. Place these in a bowl and coat them generously with vegetable oil spray. Toss

gently, then spray generously again before tossing, until all are glistening.

4. Gently pour the tofu pieces into the air fryer oven, spread them into as close to one layer as possible, and air-fry for 20 minutes, using kitchen tongs to gently rearrange the pieces at the 7- and 14-minute marks, until light brown and crisp.

5. Gently pour the tofu pieces onto a wire rack. Cool for 5 minutes before serving warm.

Italian Rice Balls

Servings: 8
Cooking Time: 10 Minutes

Ingredients:

- 1½ cups cooked sticky rice
- ½ teaspoon Italian seasoning blend
- ¾ teaspoon salt
- 8 pitted black olives
- 1 ounce mozzarella cheese cut into tiny sticks (small enough to stuff into olives)
- 2 eggs, beaten
- ⅓ cup Italian breadcrumbs
- ¾ cup panko breadcrumbs
- oil for misting or cooking spray

Directions:

1. Preheat the toaster oven to 390°F.
2. Stir together the cooked rice, Italian seasoning, and ½ teaspoon of salt.
3. Stuff each black olive with a piece of mozzarella cheese.
4. Shape the rice into a log and divide into 8 equal pieces. Using slightly damp hands, mold each portion of rice around an olive and shape into a firm ball. Chill in freezer for 10 to 15 minutes or until the outside is cold to the touch.
5. Set up 3 shallow dishes for dipping: beaten eggs in one dish, Italian breadcrumbs in another

dish, and in the third dish mix the panko crumbs and remaining salt.

6. Roll each rice ball in breadcrumbs, dip in beaten egg, and then roll in the panko crumbs.
7. Spray all sides with oil.
8. Air-fry for 10 minutes, until outside is light golden brown and crispy.

Parmesan Peas

Servings: 3
Cooking Time: 15 Minutes

Ingredients:

- 3 tablespoons olive oil
- 1 clove garlic, minced
- 1 1/2 cups frozen peas, thawed and drained
- 1/2 cup shredded Parmesan cheese
- 1/2 teaspoon coarse pepper

Directions:

1. Heat the toaster oven to 350°F.
2. In toaster oven baking pan, add oil and garlic.
3. Bake for 5 minutes or until garlic is lightly browned.
4. Add peas to the pan.
5. Bake an additional 8 to 10 minutes or until peas are heated.
6. Sprinkle with cheese and pepper before serving.

Fried Wontons

Servings: 24
Cooking Time: 6 Minutes

Ingredients:

- 6 ounces Lean ground beef, pork, or turkey
- 1 tablespoon Regular or reduced-sodium soy sauce or tamari sauce
- 1½ teaspoons Minced garlic
- ¾ teaspoon Ground dried ginger

- ½ teaspoon Ground white pepper
- 24 Wonton wrappers (thawed, if necessary)
- Vegetable oil spray

Directions:

1. Preheat the toaster oven to 350°F .

2. Stir the ground meat, soy or tamari sauce, garlic, ginger, and white pepper in a bowl until the spices are uniformly distributed in the mixture.

3. Set a small bowl of water on a clean, dry surface or next to a clean, dry cutting board. Set one wonton wrapper on the surface. Dip your clean finger in the water, then run it along the edges of the wrapper. Set 1 teaspoon of the ground meat mixture in the center of the wrapper. Fold it over, corner to corner, to create a filled triangle. Press to seal the edges, then pull the corners on the longest side up and together over the filling to create the classic wonton shape. Press the corners together to seal. Set aside and continue filling and making more filled wontons.

4. Generously coat the filled wontons on all sides with vegetable oil spray. Arrange them in the air fryer oven in one layer and air-fry for 6 minutes, at the 2- and 4-minute marks to rearrange the wontons (but always making sure they're still in one layer), until golden brown and crisp.

5. Pour the wontons in the pan onto a wire rack or even into a serving bowl. Cool for 2 or 3 minutes (but not much longer) and serve hot.

Parmesan Garlic French Fries

Servings: 4
Cooking Time: 25 Minutes

Ingredients:

- 16 ounces frozen regular-cut french fries
- 2 tablespoons olive oil

- 1 teaspoon Italian seasoning
- ½ teaspoon garlic powder
- ½ teaspoon kosher salt
- ¼ teaspoon freshly ground black pepper
- ¼ cup grated Parmesan cheese
- 2 tablespoons minced fresh flat-leaf (Italian) parsley

Directions:

1. Preheat the toaster oven to 425°F. Line a 12 x 12-inch baking pan with nonstick aluminum foil (or if lining the pan with regular foil, spray it with nonstick cooking spray).

2. Place the french fries in a large bowl. Drizzle with the olive oil and toss to coat the fries evenly.

3. Blend the Italian seasoning, garlic powder, salt, and pepper in a small bowl. Sprinkle the seasonings over the fries and toss to coat evenly. Spread the fries in a single layer in the prepared pan.

4. Bake, uncovered, for 10 minutes. Stir and bake for an additional 10 to 15 minutes, or until the fries are golden brown and crisp.

5. Remove the fries from the oven and immediately sprinkle with the Parmesan cheese and parsley. Toss gently to coat them evenly.

Creamy Scalloped Potatoes

Servings: 4
Cooking Time: 58 Minutes

Ingredients:

- Oil spray (hand-pumped)
- 2 tablespoons salted butter
- 1 small onion, finely chopped
- 1 teaspoon minced garlic
- 2 tablespoons all-purpose flour
- 1 cup whole milk
- ½ cup low-sodium chicken broth

- ¼ teaspoon ground nutmeg
- ⅛ teaspoon sea salt
- ⅛ teaspoon freshly ground black pepper
- 1½ pounds russet potatoes, cut into ⅛-inch-thick slices

Directions:

1. Place the rack on position 1 and preheat the toaster oven on BAKE to 350°F for 5 minutes.

2. Lightly spray an 8-inch-square baking dish with oil and set aside.

3. Melt the butter in a medium saucepan over medium-high heat. Sauté the onion and garlic in the butter until softened, about 4 minutes. Add the flour and cook, whisking, for 1 minute.

4. Whisk in the milk and chicken broth until well blended and cook, whisking constantly, until thickened, about 3 minutes. Remove the sauce from the heat and whisk in the nutmeg, salt, and pepper. Set aside.

5. Layer one-third of the potato slices in the baking dish and top with one-third of the sauce. Repeat the layering in thirds, ending with the cream sauce.

6. Cover the dish with aluminum foil and bake for 25 minutes. Remove the foil and bake for an additional 25 minutes until golden brown and the potatoes are tender. Serve.

Sweet Apple Fries

Servings: 3
Cooking Time: 8 Minutes

Ingredients:

- 2 Medium-size sweet apple(s), such as Gala or Fuji
- 1 Large egg white(s)
- 2 tablespoons Water

- 1½ cups Finely ground gingersnap crumbs (gluten-free, if a concern)
- Vegetable oil spray

Directions:

1. Preheat the toaster oven to 375°F .

2. Peel and core an apple, then cut it into 12 slices . Repeat with more apples as necessary.

3. Whisk the egg white(s) and water in a medium bowl until foamy. Add the apple slices and toss well to coat.

4. Spread the gingersnap crumbs across a dinner plate. Using clean hands, pick up an apple slice, let any excess egg white mixture slip back into the rest, and dredge the slice in the crumbs, coating it lightly but evenly on all sides. Set it aside and continue coating the remaining apple slices.

5. Lightly coat the slices on all sides with vegetable oil spray, then set them curved side down in the air fryer oven in one layer. Air-fry undisturbed for 6 minutes, or until browned and crisp. You may need to air-fry the slices for 2 minutes longer if the temperature is at 360°F.

6. Use kitchen tongs to transfer the slices to a wire rack. Cool for 2 to 3 minutes before serving.

Granola Three Ways

Servings: 4
Cooking Time: 10 Minutes

Ingredients:

- Nantucket Granola
- ¼ cup maple syrup
- ¼ cup dark brown sugar
- 1 tablespoon butter
- 1 teaspoon vanilla extract
- 1 cup rolled oats
- ½ cup dried cranberries
- ½ cup walnuts, chopped

- ¼ cup pumpkin seeds
- ¼ cup shredded coconut
- Blueberry Delight
- ¼ cup honey
- ¼ cup light brown sugar
- 1 tablespoon butter
- 1 teaspoon lemon extract
- 1 cup rolled oats
- ½ cup sliced almonds
- ½ cup dried blueberries
- ¼ cup pumpkin seeds
- ¼ cup sunflower seeds
- Cherry Black Forest Mix
- ¼ cup honey
- ¼ cup light brown sugar
- 1 tablespoon butter
- 1 teaspoon almond extract
- 1 cup rolled oats
- ½ cup sliced almonds
- ½ cup dried cherries
- ¼ cup shredded coconut
- ¼ cup dark chocolate chips
- oil for misting or cooking spray

Directions:

1. Combine the syrup or honey, brown sugar, and butter in a small saucepan or microwave-safe bowl. Heat and stir just until butter melts and sugar dissolves. Stir in the extract.

2. Place all other dry ingredients in a large bowl. (For the Cherry Black Forest Mix, don't add the chocolate chips yet.)

3. Pour melted butter mixture over dry ingredients and stir until oat mixture is well coated.

4. Lightly spray a baking pan with oil or cooking spray.

5. Pour granola into pan and air-fry at 390°F for 5 minutes. Stir. Continue cooking for 5 minutes, stirring every minute or two, until golden brown. Watch closely. Once the mixture begins to brown, it will cook quickly.

6. Remove granola from pan and spread on wax paper. It will become crispier as it cools.

7. For the Cherry Black Forest Mix, stir in chocolate chips after granola has cooled completely.

8. Store in an airtight container.

Fried Green Tomatoes

Servings: 4
Cooking Time: 15 Minutes

Ingredients:

- 2 eggs
- ¼ cup buttermilk
- ½ cup cornmeal
- ½ cup breadcrumbs
- ¼ teaspoon salt
- 1½ pounds firm green tomatoes, cut in ¼-inch slices
- oil for misting or cooking spray
- Horseradish Drizzle
- ¼ cup mayonnaise
- ¼ cup sour cream
- 2 teaspoons prepared horseradish
- ½ teaspoon Worcestershire sauce
- ½ teaspoon lemon juice
- ⅛ teaspoon black pepper

Directions:

1. Mix all ingredients for Horseradish Drizzle together and chill while you prepare the green tomatoes.

2. Preheat the toaster oven to 390°F.

3. Beat the eggs and buttermilk together in a shallow bowl.

4. Mix cornmeal, breadcrumbs, and salt together in a plate or shallow dish.

5. Dip 4 tomato slices in the egg mixture, then roll in the breadcrumb mixture.

6. Mist one side with oil and place in air fryer oven, oil-side down, in a single layer.

7. Mist the top with oil.

8. Air-fry for 15 minutes, turning once, until brown and crispy.

9. Repeat steps 5 through 8 to cook remaining tomatoes.

10. Drizzle horseradish sauce over tomatoes just before serving.

FISH AND SEAFOOD

Fish Sticks For Kids

Servings: 8
Cooking Time: 6 Minutes

Ingredients:
- 8 ounces fish fillets (pollock or cod)
- salt (optional)
- ½ cup plain breadcrumbs
- oil for misting or cooking spray

Directions:
1. Cut fish fillets into "fingers" about ½ x 3 inches. Sprinkle with salt to taste, if desired.
2. Roll fish in breadcrumbs. Spray all sides with oil or cooking spray.
3. Place in air fryer oven in single layer and air-fry at 390°F for 6 minutes, until golden brown and crispy.

Broiled Dill And Lemon Salmon

Servings: 25
Cooking Time: 2 Minutes

Ingredients:
- Brushing mixture:
- 2 tablespoons lemon juice
- 2 tablespoons olive oil
- 1 tablespoon soy sauce
- 1 teaspoon dried dill or dill weed
- ½ teaspoon garlic powder
- 1 teaspoon soy sauce
- 2 6-ounce salmon steaks

Directions:
1. Combine the brushing mixture ingredients in a small bowl and brush the salmon steak tops, skin side down, liberally, reserving the remaining mixture. Let the steaks sit at room temperature for 10 minutes, then place on a broiling rack with a pan underneath.
2. BROIL 15 minutes, remove from the oven, and brush the steaks with the remaining mixture. Broil again for 5 minutes, or until the meat flakes easily with a fork.

Chilled Clam Cake Slices With Dijon Dill Sauce

Servings: 6
Cooking Time: 30 Minutes

Ingredients:
- 1 10-ounce can minced clams, drained
- 1 egg
- ¾ cup multigrain bread crumbs
- 1 tablespoon vegetable oil
- 1 cup skim milk
- ¼ cup chopped onions
- 2 tablespoons chopped pimientos, drained
- Salt and freshly ground black pepper to taste
- Dijon Dill Sauce (recipe follows)

Directions:
1. Preheat the toaster oven to 400° F.
2. Combine all the ingredients in a medium bowl, mixing well. Transfer to an 8½ × 8½ × 2-inch oiled or nonstick square (cake) pan.
3. BAKE for 30 minutes, or until the top is browned. Let cool, then chill the loaf in the refrigerator. Cut into thin slices or squares and serve with the sauce.

Pecan-topped Sole

Servings: 4

Cooking Time: 12 Minutes

Ingredients:

- 4 (4-ounce) sole fillets
- Sea salt, for seasoning
- Freshly ground black pepper, for seasoning
- 1 cup crushed pecans
- ½ cup seasoned bread crumbs
- 1 large egg
- 2 tablespoons water
- Oil spray (hand-pumped)

Directions:

1. Preheat the toaster oven to 375°F on BAKE for 5 minutes.
2. Line the baking tray with parchment paper.
3. Pat the fish dry with paper towels and lightly season with salt and pepper.
4. In a small bowl, stir the pecans and bread crumbs.
5. In another small bowl, beat the egg and water until well blended.
6. Dredge the fish in the egg mixture, shaking off any excess, then in the nut mixture.
7. Place the fish in the baking sheet and repeat with the remaining fish.
8. Lightly spray the fillets with the oil on both sides.
9. In position 2, bake until golden and crispy, turning halfway, for 12 minutes in total. Serve.

Beer-breaded Halibut Fish Tacos

Servings: 4

Cooking Time: 10 Minutes

Ingredients:

- 1 pound halibut, cut into 1-inch strips
- 1 cup light beer
- 1 jalapeño, minced and divided
- 1 clove garlic, minced
- ¼ teaspoon ground cumin
- ½ cup cornmeal
- ¼ cup all-purpose flour
- 1¼ teaspoons sea salt, divided
- 2 cups shredded cabbage
- 1 lime, juiced and divided
- ¼ cup Greek yogurt
- ¼ cup mayonnaise
- 1 cup grape tomatoes, quartered
- ½ cup chopped cilantro
- ¼ cup chopped onion
- 1 egg, whisked
- 8 corn tortillas

Directions:

1. In a shallow baking dish, place the fish, the beer, 1 teaspoon of the minced jalapeño, the garlic, and the cumin. Cover and refrigerate for 30 minutes.
2. Meanwhile, in a medium bowl, mix together the cornmeal, flour, and ½ teaspoon of the salt.
3. In large bowl, mix together the shredded cabbage, 1 tablespoon of the lime juice, the Greek yogurt, the mayonnaise, and ½ teaspoon of the salt.
4. In a small bowl, make the pico de gallo by mixing together the tomatoes, cilantro, onion, ¼ teaspoon of the salt, the remaining jalapeño, and the remaining lime juice.
5. Remove the fish from the refrigerator and discard the marinade. Dredge the fish in the whisked egg; then dredge the fish in the cornmeal flour mixture, until all pieces of fish have been breaded.
6. Preheat the toaster oven to 350°F.

7. Place the fish in the air fryer oven and spray liberally with cooking spray. Air-fry for 6 minutes, flip the fish, and cook another 4 minutes.

8. While the fish is cooking, heat the tortillas in a heavy skillet for 1 to 2 minutes over high heat.

9. To assemble the tacos, place the battered fish on the heated tortillas, and top with slaw and pico de gallo. Serve immediately.

Almond-crusted Fish

Servings: 4
Cooking Time: 10 Minutes

Ingredients:

- 4 4-ounce fish fillets
- ¾ cup breadcrumbs
- ¼ cup sliced almonds, crushed
- 2 tablespoons lemon juice
- ⅛ teaspoon cayenne
- salt and pepper
- ¾ cup flour
- 1 egg, beaten with 1 tablespoon water
- oil for misting or cooking spray

Directions:

1. Split fish fillets lengthwise down the center to create 8 pieces.

2. Mix breadcrumbs and almonds together and set aside.

3. Mix the lemon juice and cayenne together. Brush on all sides of fish.

4. Season fish to taste with salt and pepper.

5. Place the flour on a sheet of wax paper.

6. Roll fillets in flour, dip in egg wash, and roll in the crumb mixture.

7. Mist both sides of fish with oil or cooking spray.

8. Spray air fryer oven and lay fillets inside.

9. Air-fry at 390°F for 5 minutes, turn fish over, and air-fry for an additional 5 minutes or until fish is done and flakes easily.

Broiled Lemon Coconut Shrimp

Servings: 4
Cooking Time: 10 Minutes

Ingredients:

- Brushing mixture:
- 2 tablespoons lemon juice
- 4 tablespoons olive oil
- 1 tablespoon grated lemon zest
- Salt to taste
- 1 pound fresh shrimp, peeled, deveined, and butterflied
- ½ cup grated unsweetened coconut

Directions:

1. Combine the brushing mixture ingredients in a small bowl. Add the shrimp and toss to coat well. Set aside.

2. Place the coconut on a plate, spreading it out evenly.

3. Press each shrimp into the coconut, coating well on all sides. Place the shrimp in an 8½ × 8½ × 2-inch oiled or nonstick square (cake) pan.

4. BROIL the shrimp for 5 minutes, turn with tongs, and broil for 5 more minutes, or until browned lightly.

Skewered Salsa Verde Shrimp

Servings: 4
Cooking Time: 8 Minutes

Ingredients:

- 1½ pounds large fresh shrimp, peeled and deveined
- Brushing mixture:
- 1 7-ounce can salsa verde

- 1 teaspoon ground cumin
- ½ teaspoon chopped fresh cilantro or parsley
- 1 teaspoon garlic powder
- 3 tablespoons plain yogurt
- 1 tablespoon olive oil
- Lemon wedges

Directions:

1. Thread the shrimp onto the skewers.
2. Combine the brushing mixture ingredients in a small bowl. Adjust the seasonings and brush the shrimp with the mixture.
3. BROIL the shrimp for 4 minutes. Turn the skewers, brush the shrimp again, and broil for another 4 minutes, or until the shrimp are firm and cooked. Remove the shrimp from the skewers and serve with lemon wedges.

Shrimp With Jalapeño Dip

Servings: 4
Cooking Time: 10 Minutes

Ingredients:

- Seasonings:
- 1 teaspoon ground cumin
- 1 tablespoon minced garlic
- 1 teaspoon paprika
- 1 teaspoon chili powder
- Pinch of cayenne
- Salt to taste
- 1½ pounds large shrimp, peeled and deveined

Directions:

1. Combine the seasonings in a plastic bag, add the shrimp, and shake well to coat. Transfer the shrimp to an oiled or nonstick 8½ × 8½ × 2-inch square baking (cake) pan.
2. BROIL for 5 minutes. Remove the pan from the oven and turn the shrimp with tongs. Broil 5 minutes again, or until the shrimp are cooked

(they should be firm but not rubbery.) Serve with Jalapeño Dip.

Miso-rubbed Salmon Fillets

Servings: 3
Cooking Time: 5 Minutes

Ingredients:

- ¼ cup White (shiro) miso paste (usually made from rice and soy beans)
- 1½ tablespoons Mirin or a substitute
- 2½ teaspoons Unseasoned rice vinegar
- Vegetable oil spray
- 3 6-ounce skin-on salmon fillets

Directions:

1. Preheat the toaster oven to 400°F.
2. Mix the miso, mirin, and vinegar in a small bowl until uniform.
3. Remove from the machine. Generously spray the skin side of each fillet. Pick them up one by one with a nonstick-safe spatula and set them in the baking pan skin side down with as much air space between them as possible. Coat the top of each fillet with the miso mixture, dividing it evenly between them.
4. Return the baking pan to the machine. Air-fry undisturbed for 5 minutes, or until lightly browned and firm.
5. Use a nonstick-safe spatula to transfer the fillets to serving plates. Cool for only a minute or so before serving.

Stuffed Baked Red Snapper

Servings: 2
Cooking Time: 30 Minutes

Ingredients:

- Stuffing mixture:

- 12 medium shrimp, cooked, peeled, and chopped
- 2 tablespoons multigrain bread crumbs
- 1 teaspoon anchovy paste
- ¼ teaspoon paprika
- Salt to taste
- 2 6-ounce red snapper fillets
- 1 egg
- ½ cup fat-free half-and-half
- 2 tablespoons cooking sherry

Directions:

1. Preheat the toaster oven to 350° F.
2. Combine all the stuffing mixture ingredients in a medium bowl and place a mound of mixture on one end of each fillet. Fold over the other fillet end, skewering the edge with toothpicks.
3. Place the rolled fillets in an oiled or nonstick 8½ × 8½ × 2-inch square baking (cake) pan.
4. Whisk the egg in a small bowl until light in color, then whisk in the half-and-half and sherry. Pour over the fillets. Cover the pan with aluminum foil.
5. BAKE for 30 minutes.

Tilapia Teriyaki

Servings: 3
Cooking Time: 10 Minutes

Ingredients:

- 4 tablespoons teriyaki sauce
- 1 tablespoon pineapple juice
- 1 pound tilapia fillets
- cooking spray
- 6 ounces frozen mixed peppers with onions, thawed and drained
- 2 cups cooked rice

Directions:

1. Mix the teriyaki sauce and pineapple juice together in a small bowl.
2. Split tilapia fillets down the center lengthwise.
3. Brush all sides of fish with the sauce, spray air fryer oven with nonstick cooking spray, and place fish in the air fryer oven.
4. Stir the peppers and onions into the remaining sauce and spoon over the fish. Save any leftover sauce for drizzling over the fish when serving.
5. Air-fry at 360°F for 10 minutes, until fish flakes easily with a fork and is done in center.
6. Divide into 3 or 4 servings and serve each with approximately ½ cup cooked rice.

Rolled Asparagus Flounder

Servings: 4
Cooking Time: 30 Minutes

Ingredients:

- 1 dozen asparagus stalks, tough stem part cut off
- 4 6-ounce flounder fillets
- 4 tablespoons chopped scallions
- 4 tablespoons shredded carrots
- 4 tablespoons finely chopped
- Almonds
- 1 teaspoon dried dill weed
- Salt and freshly ground black pepper
- 1 lemon, cut into wedges

Directions:

1. Preheat the toaster oven to 400° F.
2. Place 3 asparagus stalks lengthwise on a flounder fillet. Add 1 tablespoon scallions, 1 tablespoon carrots, 1 tablespoon almonds, and a sprinkling of dill. Season to taste with salt and pepper and roll the fillet together so that the long edges overlap. Secure the edges with toothpicks

or tie with cotton string. Carefully place the rolled fillet in an oiled or nonstick 8½ × 8½ × 2-inch square baking (cake) pan. Repeat the process for the remaining ingredients. Cover the pan with aluminum foil.

3. BAKE, covered, for 20 minutes, or until the asparagus is tender. Remove the cover.

4. BROIL, uncovered, for 10 minutes, or until the fish is lightly browned. Remove and discard the toothpicks or string. Serve the rolled filets with lemon wedges.

Mediterranean Baked Fish

Servings: 4
Cooking Time: 25 Minutes

Ingredients:

- Baking mixture:
- 1 tablespoon olive oil
- 2 tablespoons tomato paste
- 3 plum tomatoes, chopped
- 2 garlic cloves, minced
- 2 tablespoons capers
- 2 tablespoons pitted and chopped black olives
- 2 tablespoons chopped fresh basil leaves
- 2 tablespoons chopped fresh parsley
- 4 6-ounce fish fillets (red snapper, cod, whiting, sole, or mackerel)

Directions:

1. Preheat the toaster oven to 350° F.

2. Combine the baking mixture ingredients in a small bowl. Set aside.

3. Layer the fillets in an oiled or nonstick 8½ × 8½ × 2-inch square baking (cake) pan, overlapping them if necessary, and spoon the baking mixture over the fish.

4. BAKE, covered, for 25 minutes, or until the fish flakes easily with a fork.

Sweet Chili Shrimp

Servings: 4
Cooking Time: 6 Minutes

Ingredients:

- 1 pound jumbo shrimp, peeled and deveined
- ¼ cup sweet chili sauce
- 1 lime, zested and juiced
- 1 tablespoon soy sauce
- 1 tablespoon honey
- 1 tablespoon olive oil
- 1 large garlic clove, minced
- ½ teaspoon salt
- ¼ teaspoon pepper
- 1 green onion, thinly sliced, for garnish

Directions:

1. Place the shrimp in a large bowl. Whisk all the remaining ingredients except the green onion in a separate bowl.

2. Pour sauce over the shrimp and toss to coat.

3. Preheat the toaster Oven to 430°F.

4. Line the food tray with foil, place shrimp on the tray, then insert at top position in the preheated oven.

5. Select the Air Fry function, adjust time to 6 minutes, and press Start/Pause.

6. Remove shrimp and garnish with sliced green onions.

Crunchy Clam Strips

Servings: 3
Cooking Time: 8 Minutes

Ingredients:

- ½ pound Clam strips, drained
- 1 Large egg, well beaten
- ½ cup All-purpose flour
- ½ cup Yellow cornmeal

- 1½ teaspoons Table salt
- 1½ teaspoons Ground black pepper
- Up to ¾ teaspoon Cayenne
- Vegetable oil spray

Directions:

1. Preheat the toaster oven to 400°F.

2. Toss the clam strips and beaten egg in a bowl until the clams are well coated.

3. Mix the flour, cornmeal, salt, pepper, and cayenne in a large zip-closed plastic bag until well combined. Using a flatware fork or small kitchen tongs, lift the clam strips one by one out of the egg, letting any excess egg slip back into the rest. Put the strips in the bag with the flour mixture. Once all the strips are in the bag, seal it until the strips are well coated.

4. Use kitchen tongs to pick out the clam strips and lay them on a cutting board (leaving any extra flour mixture in the bag to be discarded). Coat the strips on both sides with vegetable oil spray.

5. When the machine is at temperature, spread the clam strips in the air fryer oven in one layer. They may touch in places, but try to leave as much air space as possible around them. Air-fry undisturbed for 8 minutes, or until brown and crunchy.

6. Gently dump the contents of the air fryer oven onto a serving platter. Cool for just a minute or two before serving hot.

Fish Tacos With Jalapeño-lime Sauce

Servings: 4

Cooking Time: 7 Minutes

Ingredients:

- Fish Tacos
- 1 pound fish fillets
- ¼ teaspoon cumin
- ¼ teaspoon coriander
- ⅛ teaspoon ground red pepper
- 1 tablespoon lime zest
- ¼ teaspoon smoked paprika
- 1 teaspoon oil
- cooking spray
- 6–8 corn or flour tortillas (6-inch size)
- Jalapeño-Lime Sauce
- ½ cup sour cream
- 1 tablespoon lime juice
- ¼ teaspoon grated lime zest
- ½ teaspoon minced jalapeño (flesh only)
- ¼ teaspoon cumin
- Napa Cabbage Garnish
- 1 cup shredded Napa cabbage
- ¼ cup slivered red or green bell pepper
- ¼ cup slivered onion

Directions:

1. Slice the fish fillets into strips approximately ½-inch thick.

2. Put the strips into a sealable plastic bag along with the cumin, coriander, red pepper, lime zest, smoked paprika, and oil. Massage seasonings into the fish until evenly distributed.

3. Spray air fryer oven with nonstick cooking spray and place seasoned fish inside.

4. Air-fry at 390°F for approximately 5 minutes. Distribute fish. Cook an additional 2 minutes, until fish flakes easily.

5. While the fish is cooking, prepare the Jalapeño-Lime Sauce by mixing the sour cream, lime juice, lime zest, jalapeño, and cumin together to make a smooth sauce. Set aside.

6. Mix the cabbage, bell pepper, and onion together and set aside.

7. To warm refrigerated tortillas, wrap in damp paper towels and microwave for 30 to 60 seconds.
8. To serve, spoon some of fish into a warm tortilla. Add one or two tablespoons Napa Cabbage Garnish and drizzle with Jalapeño-Lime Sauce.

Snapper With Capers And Olives

Servings: 2
Cooking Time: 10 Minutes

Ingredients:
- 2 tablespoons capers
- ¼ cup pitted and sliced black olives
- 2 tablespoons olive oil
- ½ teaspoon dried oregano
- Salt and freshly ground black pepper to taste
- 2 6-ounce red snapper fillets
- 1 tomato, cut into wedges

Directions:
1. Combine the capers, olives, olive oil, and seasonings in a bowl.
2. Place the fillets in an oiled or nonstick 8½ × 8½ × 2-inch square baking (cake) pan and spoon the caper mixture over them.
3. BROIL for 10 minutes, or until the fish flakes easily with a fork. Serve with the tomato wedges.

Sea Bass With Potato Scales And Caper Aïoli

Servings: 2
Cooking Time: 10 Minutes

Ingredients:
- 2 (6- to 8-ounce) fillets of sea bass
- salt and freshly ground black pepper
- ¼ cup mayonnaise
- 2 teaspoons finely chopped lemon zest
- 1 teaspoon chopped fresh thyme
- 2 fingerling potatoes, very thinly sliced into rounds
- olive oil
- ½ clove garlic, crushed into a paste
- 1 tablespoon capers, drained and rinsed
- 1 tablespoon olive oil
- 1 teaspoon lemon juice, to taste

Directions:
1. Preheat the toaster oven to 400°F.
2. Season the fish well with salt and freshly ground black pepper. Mix the mayonnaise, lemon zest and thyme together in a small bowl. Spread a thin layer of the mayonnaise mixture on both fillets. Start layering rows of potato slices onto the fish fillets to simulate the fish scales. The second row should overlap the first row slightly. Dabbing a little more mayonnaise along the upper edge of the row of potatoes where the next row overlaps will help the potato slices stick. Press the potatoes onto the fish to secure them well and season again with salt. Brush or spray the potato layer with olive oil.
3. Transfer the fish to the air fryer oven and air-fry for 8 to 10 minutes, depending on the thickness of your fillets. 1-inch of fish should take 10 minutes at 400°F.
4. While the fish is cooking, add the garlic, capers, olive oil and lemon juice to the remaining mayonnaise mixture to make the caper aïoli.
5. Serve the fish warm with a dollop of the aïoli on top or on the side.

Pecan-crusted Tilapia

Servings: 4
Cooking Time: 8 Minutes

Ingredients:

- 1 pound skinless, boneless tilapia filets
- ¼ cup butter, melted
- 1 teaspoon minced fresh or dried rosemary
- 1 cup finely chopped pecans
- 1 teaspoon sea salt
- ¼ teaspoon paprika
- 2 tablespoons chopped parsley
- 1 lemon, cut into wedges

Directions:

1. Pat the tilapia filets dry with paper towels.
2. Pour the melted butter over the filets and flip the filets to coat them completely.
3. In a medium bowl, mix together the rosemary, pecans, salt, and paprika.
4. Preheat the toaster oven to 350°F.
5. Place the tilapia filets into the air fryer oven and top with the pecan coating. Air-fry for 6 to 8 minutes. The fish should be firm to the touch and flake easily when fully cooked.
6. Remove the fish from the air fryer oven. Top the fish with chopped parsley and serve with lemon wedges.

Shrimp Patties

Servings: 4
Cooking Time: 10 Minutes

Ingredients:

- ½ pound shelled and deveined raw shrimp
- ¼ cup chopped red bell pepper
- ¼ cup chopped green onion
- ¼ cup chopped celery
- 2 cups cooked sushi rice
- ½ teaspoon garlic powder
- ½ teaspoon Old Bay Seasoning
- ½ teaspoon salt
- 2 teaspoons Worcestershire sauce
- ½ cup plain breadcrumbs
- oil for misting or cooking spray

Directions:

1. Finely chop the shrimp. You can do this in a food processor, but it takes only a few pulses. Be careful not to overprocess into mush.
2. Place shrimp in a large bowl and add all other ingredients except the breadcrumbs and oil. Stir until well combined.
3. Preheat the toaster oven to 390°F.
4. Shape shrimp mixture into 8 patties, no more than ½-inch thick. Roll patties in breadcrumbs and mist with oil or cooking spray.
5. Place 4 shrimp patties in air fryer oven and air-fry at 390°F for 10 minutes, until shrimp cooks through and outside is crispy.
6. Repeat step 5 to cook remaining shrimp patties.

Best-dressed Trout

Servings: 2
Cooking Time: 25 Minutes

Ingredients:

- 2 dressed trout
- 1 egg, beaten
- 2 tablespoons finely ground almonds
- 2 tablespoons unbleached flour
- 1 teaspoon paprika or smoked paprika
- Pinch of salt (optional)
- 4 lemon slices, approximately ¼ inch thick
- 1 teaspoon lemon juice

Directions:

1. Preheat the toaster oven to 400° F.

2. Brush the trout (both sides) with the beaten egg. Blend the almonds, flour, paprika, and salt in a bowl and sprinkle both sides of the trout. Insert 2 lemon slices in each trout cavity and place the trout in an oiled or nonstick 8½ × 8½ × 2-inch square baking (cake) pan.

3. BAKE for 20 minutes, or until the meat is white and firm. Remove from the oven and turn the trout carefully with a spatula.

4. BROIL for 5 minutes, or until the trout is lightly browned.

Oysters Broiled In Wine Sauce

Servings: 2
Cooking Time: 20 Minutes

Ingredients:
- Sauce:
- 2 tablespoons margarine, at room temperature
- 1 cup dry white wine
- 3 garlic cloves, minced
- Salt and freshly ground black pepper to taste
- 24 fresh oysters, shucked and drained

Directions:
1. Combine the sauce ingredients in a 1-quart 8½ × 8½ × 4-inch ovenproof baking dish and adjust the seasonings to taste.

2. BROIL the sauce for 5 minutes, remove the pan from the oven, and stir. Return to the oven and broil for another 5 minutes, or until the sauce begins to bubble. Remove from the oven and cool for 5 minutes. Add the oysters, spooning the sauce over them to cover thoroughly.

3. BROIL for 5 minutes, or until the oysters are just cooked.

Crispy Sweet-and-sour Cod Fillets

Servings: 3
Cooking Time: 12 Minutes

Ingredients:
- 1½ cups Plain panko bread crumbs (gluten-free, if a concern)
- 2 tablespoons Regular or low-fat mayonnaise (not fat-free; gluten-free, if a concern)
- ¼ cup Sweet pickle relish
- 3 4- to 5-ounce skinless cod fillets

Directions:
1. Preheat the toaster oven to 400°F.

2. Pour the bread crumbs into a shallow soup plate or a small pie plate. Mix the mayonnaise and relish in a small bowl until well combined. Smear this mixture all over the cod fillets. Set them in the crumbs and turn until evenly coated on all sides, even on the ends.

3. Set the coated cod fillets in the air fryer oven with as much air space between them as possible. They should not touch. Air-fry undisturbed for 12 minutes, or until browned and crisp.

4. Use a nonstick-safe spatula to transfer the cod pieces to a wire rack. Cool for only a minute or two before serving hot.

Light Trout Amandine

Servings: 4
Cooking Time: 15 Minutes

Ingredients:
- 1 tablespoon margarine
- ½ cup sliced almonds
- 1 tablespoon lemon juice
- 1 teaspoon Worcestershire sauce
- Salt and freshly ground black pepper

- 4 6-ounce trout fillets
- 2 tablespoons chopped fresh parsley

Directions:

1. Combine the margarine and almonds in an oiled or nonstick 8½ × 8½ × 2-inch square baking (cake) pan.

2. BROIL for 5 minutes, or until the margarine is melted. Remove the pan from the oven and add the lemon juice and Worcestershire sauce. Season to taste with salt and pepper, and stir again to blend well. Add the trout fillets and spoon the mixture over them to coat well.

3. BROIL for 10 minutes, or until the almonds and fillets are lightly browned. Garnish with the chopped parsley before serving.

Coconut Jerk Shrimp

Servings: 3
Cooking Time: 8 Minutes

Ingredients:

- 1 Large egg white(s)
- 1 teaspoon Purchased or homemade jerk dried seasoning blend
- ¾ cup Plain panko bread crumbs (gluten-free, if a concern)
- ¾ cup Unsweetened shredded coconut
- 12 Large shrimp (20–25 per pound), peeled and deveined
- Coconut oil spray

Directions:

1. Preheat the toaster oven to 375°F .

2. Whisk the egg white(s) and seasoning blend in a bowl until foamy. Add the shrimp and toss well to coat evenly.

3. Mix the bread crumbs and coconut on a dinner plate until well combined. Use kitchen tongs to pick up a shrimp, letting the excess egg white mixture slip back into the rest. Set the shrimp in the bread-crumb mixture. Turn several times to coat evenly and thoroughly. Set on a cutting board and continue coating the remainder of the shrimp.

4. Lightly coat all the shrimp on both sides with the coconut oil spray. Set them in the air fryer oven in one layer with as much space between them as possible. (You can even stand some up along the air fryer oven's wall in some models.) Air-fry undisturbed for 6 minutes, or until the coating is lightly browned. If the air fryer oven is at 360°F, you may need to add 2 minutes to the cooking time.

5. Use clean kitchen tongs to transfer the shrimp to a wire rack. Cool for only a minute or two before serving.

Tasty Fillets With Poblano Sauce

Servings: 2
Cooking Time: 20 Minutes

Ingredients:

- 4 5-ounce thin fish fillets—perch, scrod, catfish, or flounder
- 1 tablespoon olive oil
- Poblano sauce:
- 1 poblano chili, seeded and chopped
- 1 bell pepper, seeded and chopped
- 2 tablespoons chopped onion
- 5 garlic cloves, peeled
- 1 tablespoon flour
- 1 cup fat-free half-and-half
- Salt to taste

Directions:

1. Preheat the toaster oven to 350° F.

2. Brush the fillets with olive oil and transfer to an oiled or nonstick 8½ × 8½ × 2-inch square baking (cake) pan. Set aside.

3. Combine the poblano sauce ingredients and process in a blender or food processor until smooth. Spoon the poblano sauce over the fillets, covering them well.

4. BAKE, uncovered, for 20 minutes, or until the fish flakes easily with a fork.

Beer-battered Cod

Servings: 3

Cooking Time: 12 Minutes

Ingredients:

- 1½ cups All-purpose flour
- 3 tablespoons Old Bay seasoning
- 1 Large egg(s)
- ¼ cup Amber beer, pale ale, or IPA
- 3 4-ounce skinless cod fillets
- Vegetable oil spray

Directions:

1. Preheat the toaster oven to 400°F.

2. Set up and fill two shallow soup plates or small pie plates on your counter: one with the flour, whisked with the Old Bay until well combined; and one with the egg(s), whisked with the beer until foamy and uniform.

3. Dip a piece of cod in the flour mixture, turning it to coat on all sides (not just the top and bottom). Gently shake off any excess flour and dip the fish in the egg mixture, turning it to coat. Let any excess egg mixture slip back into the rest, then set the fish back in the flour mixture and coat it again, then back in the egg mixture for a second wash, then back in the flour mixture for a third time. Coat the fish on all sides with vegetable oil spray and set it aside. "Batter" the remaining piece(s) of cod in the same way.

4. Set the coated cod fillets in the air fryer oven with as much space between them as possible. They should not touch. Air-fry undisturbed for 12 minutes, or until brown and crisp.

5. Use kitchen tongs to gently transfer the fish to a wire rack. Cool for only a couple of minutes before serving.

BEEF PORK AND LAMB

Chicken Fried Steak

Servings: 4
Cooking Time: 15 Minutes

Ingredients:

- 2 eggs
- ½ cup buttermilk
- 1½ cups flour
- ¾ teaspoon salt
- ½ teaspoon pepper
- 1 pound beef cube steaks
- salt and pepper
- oil for misting or cooking spray

Directions:

1. Beat together eggs and buttermilk in a shallow dish.
2. In another shallow dish, stir together the flour, ½ teaspoon salt, and ¼ teaspoon pepper.
3. Season cube steaks with remaining salt and pepper to taste. Dip in flour, buttermilk egg wash, and then flour again.
4. Spray both sides of steaks with oil or cooking spray.
5. Cooking in 2 batches, place steaks in air fryer oven in single layer. Air-fry at 360°F for 10 minutes. Spray tops of steaks with oil and cook 5 minutes or until meat is well done.
6. Repeat to cook remaining steaks.

Almond And Sun-dried Tomato Crusted Pork Chops

Servings: 4
Cooking Time: 10 Minutes

Ingredients:

- ½ cup oil-packed sun-dried tomatoes
- ½ cup toasted almonds
- ¼ cup grated Parmesan cheese
- ½ cup olive oil
- 2 tablespoons water
- ½ teaspoon salt
- freshly ground black pepper
- 4 center-cut boneless pork chops (about 1¼ pounds)

Directions:

1. Place the sun-dried tomatoes into a food processor and pulse them until they are coarsely chopped. Add the almonds, Parmesan cheese, olive oil, water, salt and pepper. Process all the ingredients into a smooth paste. Spread most of the paste (leave a little in reserve) onto both sides of the pork chops and then pierce the meat several times with a needle-style meat tenderizer or a fork. Let the pork chops sit and marinate for at least 1 hour (refrigerate if marinating for longer than 1 hour).
2. Preheat the toaster oven to 370°F.
3. Brush a little olive oil on the bottom of the air fryer oven. Transfer the pork chops into the air fryer oven, spooning a little more of the sun-dried tomato paste onto the pork chops if there are any gaps where the paste may have been rubbed off. Air-fry the pork chops at 370°F for 10 minutes, turning the chops over halfway through the cooking process.
4. When the pork chops have finished cooking, transfer them to a serving plate and serve with mashed potatoes and vegetables for a hearty meal.

Minted Lamb Chops

Servings: 4

Cooking Time: 15 Minutes

Ingredients:
- Mint mixture:
- 4 tablespoons finely chopped fresh mint
- 2 tablespoons nonfat yogurt
- 1 tablespoon olive oil
- Salt and freshly ground black pepper to taste
- 4 lean lamb chops, fat trimmed, approximately ¾ inch thick
- 1 tablespoon balsamic vinegar

Directions:
1. Combine the mint mixture ingredients in a small bowl, stirring well to blend. Set aside. Place the lamp chops on a broiling rack with a pan underneath.
2. BROIL the lamb chops for 10 minutes, or until they are slightly pink. Remove from the oven and brush one side liberally with balsamic vinegar. Turn the chops over with tongs and spread with the mint mixture, using all of the mixture.
3. BROIL again for 5 minutes, or until lightly browned.

Red Curry Flank Steak

Servings: 4

Cooking Time: 18 Minutes

Ingredients:
- 3 tablespoons red curry paste
- ¼ cup olive oil
- 2 teaspoons grated fresh ginger
- 2 tablespoons soy sauce
- 2 tablespoons rice wine vinegar
- 3 scallions, minced
- 1½ pounds flank steak
- fresh cilantro (or parsley) leaves

Directions:
1. Mix the red curry paste, olive oil, ginger, soy sauce, rice vinegar and scallions together in a bowl. Place the flank steak in a shallow glass dish and pour half the marinade over the steak. Pierce the steak several times with a fork or meat tenderizer to let the marinade penetrate the meat. Turn the steak over, pour the remaining marinade over the top and pierce the steak several times again. Cover and marinate the steak in the refrigerator for 6 to 8 hours.
2. When you are ready to cook, remove the steak from the refrigerator and let it sit at room temperature for 30 minutes.
3. Preheat the toaster oven to 400°F.
4. Cut the flank steak in half so that it fits more easily into the air fryer oven and transfer both pieces to the air fryer oven. Pour the marinade over the steak. Air-fry for 18 minutes, depending on your preferred degree of doneness of the steak (12 minutes = medium rare). Flip the steak over halfway through the cooking time.
5. When your desired degree of doneness has been reached, remove the steak to a cutting board and let it rest for 5 minutes before slicing. Thinly slice the flank steak against the grain of the meat. Transfer the slices to a serving platter, pour any juice from the bottom of the air fryer oven over the sliced flank steak and sprinkle the fresh cilantro on top.

Classic Pepperoni Pizza

Servings: 4
Cooking Time: 11 Minutes

Ingredients:

- Oil spray (hand-pumped)
- 1 pound premade pizza dough, or your favorite recipe
- ½ cup store-bought pizza sauce
- ¼ cup grated Parmesan cheese
- ¾ cup shredded mozzarella
- 10 to 12 slices pepperoni
- 2 tablespoons chopped fresh basil
- Pinch red pepper flakes

Directions:

1. Preheat the toaster oven to 425°F on BAKE for 5 minutes.
2. Spray the baking tray with the oil and spread the pizza dough with your fingertips so that it covers the tray. Prick the dough with a fork.
3. In position 2, bake for 8 minutes until the crust is lightly golden.
4. Take the crust out and spread with the pizza sauce, leaving a ½-inch border around the edge. Sprinkle with Parmesan and mozzarella cheeses and arrange the pepperoni on the pizza.
5. Bake for 3 minutes until the cheese is melted and bubbly.
6. Top with the basil and red pepper flakes and serve.

Pretzel-coated Pork Tenderloin

Servings: 4
Cooking Time: 10 Minutes

Ingredients:

- 1 Large egg white(s)
- 2 teaspoons Dijon mustard (gluten-free, if a concern)
- 1½ cups (about 6 ounces) Crushed pretzel crumbs
- 1 pound (4 sections) Pork tenderloin, cut into ¼-pound (4-ounce) sections
- Vegetable oil spray

Directions:

1. Preheat the toaster oven to 350°F .
2. Set up and fill two shallow soup plates or small pie plates on your counter: one for the egg white(s), whisked with the mustard until foamy; and one for the pretzel crumbs.
3. Dip a section of pork tenderloin in the egg white mixture and turn it to coat well, even on the ends. Let any excess egg white mixture slip back into the rest, then set the pork in the pretzel crumbs. Roll it several times, pressing gently, until the pork is evenly coated, even on the ends. Generously coat the pork section with vegetable oil spray, set it aside, and continue coating and spraying the remaining sections.
4. Set the pork sections in the air fryer oven with at least ¼ inch between them. Air-fry undisturbed for 10 minutes, or until an instant-read meat thermometer inserted into the center of one section registers 145°F.
5. Use kitchen tongs to transfer the pieces to a wire rack. Cool for 3 to 5 minutes before serving.

Stuffed Pork Chops

Servings: 4
Cooking Time: 12 Minutes

Ingredients:

- 4 boneless pork chops
- ½ teaspoon salt
- ½ teaspoon black pepper

- ¼ teaspoon paprika
- 1 cup frozen spinach, defrosted and squeezed dry
- 2 cloves garlic, minced
- 2 ounces cream cheese
- ¼ cup grated Parmesan cheese
- 1 tablespoon extra-virgin olive oil

Directions:

1. Pat the pork chops with a paper towel. Make a slit in the side of each pork chop to create a pouch.

2. Season the pork chops with the salt, pepper, and paprika.

3. In a small bowl, mix together the spinach, garlic, cream cheese, and Parmesan cheese.

4. Divide the mixture into fourths and stuff the pork chop pouches. Secure the pouches with toothpicks.

5. Preheat the toaster oven to 400°F.

6. Place the stuffed pork chops in the air fryer oven and spray liberally with cooking spray. Air-fry for 6 minutes, flip and coat with more cooking spray, and cook another 6 minutes. Check to make sure the meat is cooked to an internal temperature of 145°F. Cook the pork chops in batches, as needed.

Lamb Burger With Feta And Olives

Servings: 3
Cooking Time: 16 Minutes

Ingredients:

- 2 teaspoons olive oil
- ⅓ onion, finely chopped
- 1 clove garlic, minced
- 1 pound ground lamb
- 2 tablespoons fresh parsley, finely chopped

- 1½ teaspoons fresh oregano, finely chopped
- ½ cup black olives, finely chopped
- ⅓ cup crumbled feta cheese
- ½ teaspoon salt
- freshly ground black pepper
- 4 thick pita breads
- toppings and condiments

Directions:

1. Preheat a medium skillet over medium-high heat on the stovetop. Add the olive oil and cook the onion until tender, but not browned – about 4 to 5 minutes. Add the garlic and air-fry for another minute. Transfer the onion and garlic to a mixing bowl and add the ground lamb, parsley, oregano, olives, feta cheese, salt and pepper. Gently mix the ingredients together.

2. Divide the mixture into 3 or 4 equal portions and then form the hamburgers, being careful not to over-handle the meat. One good way to do this is to throw the meat back and forth between your hands like a baseball, packing the meat each time you catch it. Flatten the balls into patties, making an indentation in the center of each patty. Flatten the sides of the patties as well to make it easier to fit them into the air fryer oven.

3. Preheat the toaster oven to 370°F.

4. If you don't have room for all four burgers, air-fry two or three burgers at a time for 8 minutes at 370°F. Flip the burgers over and air-fry for another 8 minutes. If you cooked your burgers in batches, return the first batch of burgers to the air fryer oven for the last two minutes of cooking to re-heat. This should give you a medium-well burger. If you'd prefer a medium-rare burger, shorten the cooking time to about 13 minutes. Remove the burgers to a

resting plate and let the burgers rest for a few minutes before dressing and serving.

5. While the burgers are resting, toast the pita breads in the air fryer oven for 2 minutes. Tuck the burgers into the toasted pita breads, or wrap the pitas around the burgers and serve with a tzatziki sauce or some mayonnaise.

Steak Pinwheels With Pepper Slaw And Minneapolis Potato Salad

Servings: 4
Cooking Time: 16 Minutes

Ingredients:
- Brushing mixture:
- ½ cup cold strong brewed coffee
- 2 tablespoons molasses
- 1 tablespoon tomato paste
- 2 garlic cloves, minced
- 1 tablespoon olive oil
- Garlic powder
- 1 teaspoon butcher's pepper
- 1 pound lean, boneless beefsteak, flattened to ⅛-inch thickness with a meat mallet or rolling pin (place steak between 2 sheets of heavy-duty plastic wrap)

Directions:
1. Combine the brushing mixture ingredients in a small bowl and set aside.
2. Cut the steak into 2 × 3-inch strips, brush with the mixture, and roll up, securing the edges with toothpicks. Brush again with the mixture and place in an oiled or nonstick 8½ × 8½ × 2-inch square baking (cake) pan.

3. BROIL for 8 minutes, then turn with tongs, brush with the mixture again, and broil for another 8 minutes, or until browned.

Lamb Curry

Servings: 4
Cooking Time: 40 Minutes

Ingredients:
- 1 pound lean lamb for stewing, trimmed and cut into 1 × 1-inch pieces
- 1 small onion, chopped
- 3 garlic cloves, minced
- 2 plum tomatoes, chopped
- ½ cup dry white wine
- 2 tablespoons curry powder
- Salt and cayenne to taste

Directions:
1. Preheat the toaster oven to 400° F.
2. Combine all the ingredients in an 8½ × 8½ × 4-inch ovenproof baking dish. Adjust the seasonings.
3. BAKE, covered, for 40 minutes, or until the meat is tender and the onion is cooked.

Beef Vegetable Stew

Servings: 4
Cooking Time: 120 Minutes

Ingredients:
- 1 pound lean stewing beef, cut into 1-inch chunks
- 2 carrots, diced
- 2 celery stalks
- 1 large potato, diced
- ½ sweet onion, chopped
- 2 teaspoons minced garlic
- 1 (15-ounce) can diced tomatoes, with juices
- 1 teaspoon sea salt

- ½ teaspoon freshly ground black pepper
- 1 cup low-sodium beef broth
- 3 tablespoons all-purpose flour
- 1 cup frozen peas

Directions:

1. Place the rack in position 1 and preheat the toaster oven to 375°F on BAKE for 5 minutes.

2. In a 1½-quart casserole dish, combine the beef, carrots, celery, potato, onion, garlic, tomatoes, salt, and pepper.

3. In a small bowl, stir the broth and flour until well combined. Add the broth mixture to the beef mixture and stir to combine.

4. Cover with foil or a lid and bake for 2 hours, stirring each time you reset the timer, until the meat is very tender.

5. Stir in the peas and let stand for 10 minutes. Serve.

Italian Sausage & Peppers

Servings: 6
Cooking Time: 25 Minutes

Ingredients:

- 1 6-ounce can tomato paste
- ⅔ cup water
- 1 8-ounce can tomato sauce
- 1 teaspoon dried parsley flakes
- ½ teaspoon garlic powder
- ⅛ teaspoon oregano
- ½ pound mild Italian bulk sausage
- 1 tablespoon extra virgin olive oil
- ½ large onion, cut in 1-inch chunks
- 4 ounces fresh mushrooms, sliced
- 1 large green bell pepper, cut in 1-inch chunks
- 8 ounces spaghetti, cooked
- Parmesan cheese for serving

Directions:

1. In a large saucepan or skillet, stir together the tomato paste, water, tomato sauce, parsley, garlic, and oregano. Heat on stovetop over very low heat while preparing meat and vegetables.

2. Break sausage into small chunks, about ½-inch pieces. Place in air fryer oven baking pan.

3. Air-fry at 390°F for 5 minutes. Stir. Cook 7 minutes longer or until sausage is well done. Remove from pan, drain on paper towels, and add to the sauce mixture.

4. If any sausage grease remains in baking pan, pour it off or use paper towels to soak it up. (Be careful handling that hot pan!)

5. Place olive oil, onions, and mushrooms in pan and stir. Air-fry for 5 minutes or just until tender. Using a slotted spoon, transfer onions and mushrooms from baking pan into the sauce and sausage mixture.

6. Place bell pepper chunks in air fryer oven baking pan and air-fry for 8 minutes or until tender. When done, stir into sauce with sausage and other vegetables.

7. Serve over cooked spaghetti with plenty of Parmesan cheese.

Seasoned Boneless Pork Sirloin Chops

Servings: 2
Cooking Time: 16 Minutes

Ingredients:

- Seasoning mixture:
- ½ teaspoon ground cumin
- ¼ teaspoon turmeric
- Pinch of ground cardamom
- Pinch of grated nutmeg
- 1 teaspoon vegetable oil

- 1 teaspoon Pickapeppa sauce
- 2½- to ¾-pound boneless lean pork sirloin chops

Directions:

1. Combine the seasoning mixture ingredients in a small bowl and brush on both sides of the chops. Place the chops on the broiling rack with a pan underneath.

2. BROIL 8 minutes, remove the chops, turn, and brush with the mixture. Broil again for 8 minutes, or until the chops are done to your preference.

Chinese Pork And Vegetable Non-stir-fry

Servings: 4
Cooking Time: 30 Minutes

Ingredients:

- Seasoning sauce:
- 1 tablespoon soy sauce
- ¼ cup dry white wine
- 1 tablespoon sesame oil
- 1 tablespoon vegetable oil
- 1 teaspoon Chinese five-spice powder
- 2 6-ounce lean boneless pork chops cut into ¼ × 2-inch strips
- 1 1-pound package frozen vegetable mix or 2 cups sliced assorted fresh vegetables: broccoli, carrots, cauliflower, bell pepper, and the like
- 1 4-ounce can mushroom pieces, drained, or ½ cup cleaned and sliced fresh mushrooms
- 2 tablespoons sesame seeds
- 2 tablespoons minced fresh garlic

Directions:

1. Whisk together the seasoning sauce ingredients in a small bowl. Set aside.

2. Combine the pork, vegetables, mushrooms, sesame seeds, and garlic in an oiled or nonstick 8½ × 8½ × 2-inch square baking (cake) pan. Add the seasoning sauce ingredients and toss to coat the pork, vegetables, and mushrooms well.

3. BROIL for 30 minutes, turning with tongs every 8 minutes, until the vegetables and meat are well cooked and lightly browned.

Lamb Koftas Meatballs

Servings: 3
Cooking Time: 8 Minutes

Ingredients:

- 1 pound ground lamb
- 1 teaspoon ground cumin
- 1 teaspoon ground coriander
- 2 tablespoons chopped fresh mint
- 1 egg, beaten
- ½ teaspoon salt
- freshly ground black pepper

Directions:

1. Combine all ingredients in a bowl and mix together well. Divide the mixture into 10 portions. Roll each portion into a ball and then by cupping the meatball in your hand, shape it into an oval.

2. Preheat the toaster oven to 400°F.

3. Air-fry the koftas for 8 minutes.

4. Serve warm with the cucumber-yogurt dip.

Sweet Potato–crusted Pork Rib Chops

Servings: 2
Cooking Time: 14 Minutes

Ingredients:

- 2 Large egg white(s), well beaten

- 1½ cups (about 6 ounces) Crushed sweet potato chips (certified gluten-free, if a concern)
- 1 teaspoon Ground cinnamon
- 1 teaspoon Ground dried ginger
- 1 teaspoon Table salt (optional)
- 2 10-ounce, 1-inch-thick bone-in pork rib chop(s)

Directions:

1. Preheat the toaster oven to 375°F .
2. Set up and fill two shallow soup plates or small pie plates on your counter: one for the beaten egg white(s); and one for the crushed chips, mixed with the cinnamon, ginger, and salt (if using).
3. Dip a chop in the egg white(s), coating it on both sides as well as the edges. Let the excess egg white slip back into the rest, then set it in the crushed chip mixture. Turn it several times, pressing gently, until evenly coated on both sides and the edges. If necessary, set the chop aside and coat the remaining chop(s).
4. Set the chop(s) in the air fryer oven with as much air space between them as possible. Air-fry undisturbed for 12 minutes, or until crunchy and browned and an instant-read meat thermometer inserted into the center of a chop (without touching bone) registers 145°F. If the machine is at 360°F, you may need to add 2 minutes to the cooking time.
5. Use kitchen tongs to transfer the chop(s) to a wire rack. Cool for 2 or 3 minutes before serving.

Slow Cooked Carnitas

Servings: 6
Cooking Time: 360 Minutes

Ingredients:
- 1 pork shoulder (5 pounds), bone-in

- 2½ teaspoons kosher salt
- 1½ teaspoons black pepper
- 1½ teaspoons ground cumin
- 1 teaspoon dried oregano
- ¼ teaspoon ground coriander
- 2 bay leaves
- 6 garlic cloves
- 1 small onion, quartered
- 1 cinnamon stick
- 1 full orange peel (no white)
- 2 oranges, juiced
- 1 lime, juiced

Directions:

1. Season the pork shoulder with salt, pepper, cumin, oregano, and coriander.
2. Place the seasoned pork shoulder in a large pot along with any seasoning that did not stick to the pork.
3. Add in the bay leaves, garlic cloves, onion, cinnamon stick, and orange peel.
4. Squeeze in the juice of two oranges and one lime and cover with foil.
5. Insert the wire rack at low position in the Air Fryer Toaster Oven, then place the pot on the rack.
6. Select the Slow Cook function and press Start/Pause.
7. Remove carefully when done, uncover, and remove the bone.
8. Shred the carnitas and use them in tacos, burritos, or any other way you please.

Bourbon Broiled Steak

Servings: 2
Cooking Time: 14 Minutes

Ingredients:
- Brushing mixture:

- ¼ cup bourbon
- 1 teaspoon garlic powder
- 1 tablespoon olive oil
- 1 teaspoon soy sauce
- 2 6- to 8-ounce sirloin steaks, ¾ inch thick

Directions:

1. Combine the brushing mixture ingredients in a small bowl. Brush the steaks on both sides with the mixture and place on the broiling rack with a pan underneath.

2. BROIL 4 minutes, remove from the oven, turn with tongs, brush the top and sides, and broil again for 4 minutes, or until done to your preference. To use the brushing mixture as a sauce or gravy, pour the mixture into a baking pan.

3. BROIL the mixture for 6 minutes, or until it begins to bubble.

Ribeye Steak With Blue Cheese Compound Butter

Servings: 2
Cooking Time: 12 Minutes

Ingredients:

- 5 tablespoons unsalted butter, softened
- ¼ cup crumbled blue cheese 2 teaspoons lemon juice
- 1 tablespoon freshly chopped chives
- Salt & freshly ground black pepper, to taste
- 2 (12 ounce) boneless ribeye steaks

Directions:

1. Mix together butter, blue cheese, lemon juice, and chives until smooth.

2. Season the butter to taste with salt and pepper.

3. Place the butter on plastic wrap and form into a 3-inch log, tying the ends of the plastic wrap together.

4. Place the butter in the fridge for 4 hours to harden.

5. Allow the steaks to sit at room temperature for 1 hour.

6. Pat the steaks dry with paper towels and season to taste with salt and pepper.

7. Insert the fry basket at top position in the Cosori Smart Air Fryer Toaster Oven.

8. Preheat the toaster Oven to 450°F.

9. Place the steaks in the fry basket in the preheated oven.

10. Select the Broil function, adjust time to 12 minutes, and press Start/Pause.

11. Remove when done and allow to rest for 5 minutes.

12. Remove the butter from the fridge, unwrap, and slice into ¾-inch pieces.

13. Serve the steak with one or two pieces of sliced compound butter.

Calzones South Of The Border

Servings: 8
Cooking Time: 8 Minutes

Ingredients:

- Filling
- ¼ pound ground pork sausage
- ½ teaspoon chile powder
- ¼ teaspoon ground cumin
- ⅛ teaspoon garlic powder
- ⅛ teaspoon onion powder
- ⅛ teaspoon oregano
- ½ cup ricotta cheese
- 1 ounce sharp Cheddar cheese, shredded
- 2 ounces Pepper Jack cheese, shredded
- 1 4-ounce can chopped green chiles, drained
- oil for misting or cooking spray
- salsa, sour cream, or guacamole

- Crust
- 2 cups white wheat flour, plus more for kneading and rolling
- 1 package (¼ ounce) RapidRise yeast
- 1 teaspoon salt
- ½ teaspoon chile powder
- ½ teaspoon ground cumin
- 1 cup warm water (115°F to 125°F)
- 2 teaspoons olive oil

Directions:

1. Crumble sausage into air fryer oven baking pan and stir in the filling seasonings: chile powder, cumin, garlic powder, onion powder, and oregano. Air-fry at 390°F for 2 minutes. Stir, breaking apart, and air-fry for 3 to 4 minutes, until well done. Remove and set aside on paper towels to drain.

2. To make dough, combine flour, yeast, salt, chile powder, and cumin. Stir in warm water and oil until soft dough forms. Turn out onto lightly floured board and knead for 3 or 4 minutes. Let dough rest for 10 minutes.

3. Place the three cheeses in a medium bowl. Add cooked sausage and chiles and stir until well mixed.

4. Cut dough into 8 pieces.

5. Working with 4 pieces of the dough, press each into a circle about 5 inches in diameter. Top each dough circle with 2 heaping tablespoons of filling. Fold over into a half-moon shape and press edges together. Seal edges firmly to prevent leakage. Spray both sides with oil or cooking spray.

6. Place 4 calzones in air fryer oven and air-fry at 360°F for 5 minutes. Mist with oil or spray and air-fry for 3 minutes, until crust is done and nicely browned.

7. While the first batch is cooking, press out the remaining dough, fill, and shape into calzones.

8. Spray both sides with oil or cooking spray and air-fry for 5 minutes. If needed, mist with oil and continue cooking for 3 minutes longer. This second batch will cook a little faster than the first because your air fryer oven is already hot.

9. Serve plain or with salsa, sour cream, or guacamole.

Pesto Pork Chops

Servings: 2
Cooking Time: 15 Minutes

Ingredients:
- 2 (6-ounce) boneless pork loin chops
- 2 tablespoons basil pesto

Directions:

1. Preheat the toaster oven to 375°F on AIR FRY for 5 minutes.

2. Rub the pork chops all over with the pesto and set aside for 15 minutes.

3. Place the air-fryer basket in the baking tray and arrange the pork in the basket with no overlap.

4. In position 2, air fry for 15 minutes, turning halfway through, until the chops are lightly browned and have an internal temperature of 145°F.

5. Let the meat rest for 10 minutes and serve.

Italian Meatballs

Servings: 4
Cooking Time: 12 Minutes

Ingredients:
- 12 ounces lean ground beef
- 4 ounces Italian sausage, casing removed
- ½ cup breadcrumbs

- 1 cup grated Parmesan cheese
- 1 egg
- 2 tablespoons milk
- 2 teaspoons Italian seasoning
- ½ teaspoon onion powder
- ½ teaspoon garlic powder
- Pinch of red pepper flakes

Directions:

1. In a large bowl, place all the ingredients and mix well. Roll out 24 meatballs.

2. Preheat the toaster oven to 360°F.

3. Place the meatballs in the air fryer oven and air-fry for 12 minutes, tossing every 4 minutes. Using a food thermometer, check to ensure the internal temperature of the meatballs is 165°F.

Better-than-chinese-take-out Pork Ribs

Servings: 3
Cooking Time: 35 Minutes

Ingredients:

- 1½ tablespoons Hoisin sauce (gluten-free, if a concern)
- 1½ tablespoons Regular or low-sodium soy sauce or gluten-free tamari sauce
- 1½ tablespoons Shaoxing (Chinese cooking rice wine), dry sherry, or white grape juice
- 1½ teaspoons Minced garlic
- ¾ teaspoon Ground dried ginger
- ¾ teaspoon Ground white pepper
- 1½ pounds Pork baby back rib rack(s), cut into 2-bone pieces

Directions:

1. Mix the hoisin sauce, soy or tamari sauce, Shaoxing or its substitute, garlic, ginger, and white pepper in a large bowl. Add the rib sections and stir well to coat. Cover and refrigerate for at least 2 hours or up to 24 hours, stirring the rib sections in the marinade occasionally.

2. Preheat the toaster oven to 350°F . Set the ribs in their bowl on the counter as the machine heats.

3. When the machine is at temperature, set the rib pieces on their sides in a single layer in the air fryer oven with as much air space between them as possible. Air-fry for 35 minutes, turning and rearranging the pieces once, until deeply browned and sizzling.

4. Use kitchen tongs to transfer the rib pieces to a large serving bowl or platter. Wait a minute or two before serving them so the meat can reabsorb some of its own juices.

Kielbasa Sausage With Pierogies And Caramelized Onions

Servings: 3
Cooking Time: 30 Minutes

Ingredients:

- 1 Vidalia or sweet onion, sliced
- olive oil
- salt and freshly ground black pepper
- 2 tablespoons butter, cut into small cubes
- 1 teaspoon sugar
- 1 pound light Polish kielbasa sausage, cut into 2-inch chunks
- 1 (13-ounce) package frozen mini pierogies
- 2 teaspoons vegetable or olive oil
- chopped scallions

Directions:

1. Preheat the toaster oven to 400°F.

2. Toss the sliced onions with a little olive oil, salt and pepper and transfer them to the air fryer oven. Dot the onions with pieces of butter and

air-fry at 400°F for 2 minutes. Then sprinkle the sugar over the onions and stir. Pour any melted butter from the bottom of the air fryer oven over the onions (do this over the sink – some of the butter will spill through the pan). Continue to air-fry for another 13 minutes, stirring the pan every few minutes to cook the onions evenly.

3. Add the kielbasa chunks to the onions and toss. Air-fry for another 5 minutes. Transfer the kielbasa and onions to a bowl and cover with aluminum foil to keep warm.

4. Toss the frozen pierogies with the vegetable or olive oil and transfer them to the air fryer oven. Air-fry at 400°F for 8 minutes.

5. When the pierogies have finished cooking, return the kielbasa and onions to the air fryer oven and gently toss with the pierogies. Air-fry for 2 more minutes and then transfer everything to a serving platter. Garnish with the chopped scallions and serve hot with the spicy sour cream sauce below.

6. Kielbasa Sausage with Pierogies and Caramelized Onions

Cilantro-crusted Flank Steak

Servings: 2
Cooking Time: 16 Minutes

Ingredients:

- Coating:
- 2 tablespoons chopped onion
- 1 tablespoon olive oil
- 2 tablespoons plain nonfat yogurt
- 1 plum tomato
- ½ cup fresh cilantro leaves
- 2 tablespoons cooking sherry
- ¼ teaspoon hot sauce
- 1 teaspoon garlic powder

- ½ teaspoon chili powder
- Salt and freshly ground black pepper
- 2 8-ounce flank steaks

Directions:

1. Process the coating ingredients in a blender or food processor until smooth. Spread half of the coating mixture on top of the flank steaks. Place the steaks on a broiling rack with a pan underneath.

2. BROIL for 8 minutes. Turn with tongs, spread the remaining mixture on the steaks, and broil again for 8 minutes, or until done to your preference.

Albóndigas

Servings: 4
Cooking Time: 15 Minutes

Ingredients:

- 1 pound Lean ground pork
- 3 tablespoons Very finely chopped trimmed scallions
- 3 tablespoons Finely chopped fresh cilantro leaves
- 3 tablespoons Plain panko bread crumbs (gluten-free, if a concern)
- 3 tablespoons Dry white wine, dry sherry, or unsweetened apple juice
- 1½ teaspoons Minced garlic
- 1¼ teaspoons Mild smoked paprika
- ¾ teaspoon Dried oregano
- ¾ teaspoon Table salt
- ¼ teaspoon Ground black pepper
- Olive oil spray

Directions:

1. Preheat the toaster oven to 400°F.

2. Mix the ground pork, scallions, cilantro, bread crumbs, wine or its substitute, garlic,

smoked paprika, oregano, salt, and pepper in a bowl until the herbs and spices are evenly distributed in the mixture.

3. Lightly coat your clean hands with olive oil spray, then form the ground pork mixture into balls, using 2 tablespoons for each one. Spray your hands frequently so that the meat mixture doesn't stick.

4. Set the balls in the air fryer oven so that they're not touching, even if they're close together. Air-fry undisturbed for 15 minutes, or until well browned and an instant-read meat thermometer inserted into one or two balls registers 165°F.

5. Use a nonstick-safe spatula and kitchen tongs for balance to gently transfer the fragile balls to a wire rack to cool for 5 minutes before serving.

Barbecued Broiled Pork Chops

Servings: 2
Cooking Time: 16 Minutes

Ingredients:

- Barbecue sauce mixture:
- 1 tablespoon ketchup
- ¼ cup dry red wine
- 1 tablespoon vegetable oil
- ⅛ teaspoon smoked flavoring (liquid smoke)
- 1 teaspoon chili powder
- 1 teaspoon ground cumin
- 1 teaspoon brown sugar
- ¼ teaspoon butcher's pepper
- 2 large (6- to 8-ounce) lean pork chops, approximately ¾ to 1 inch thick

Directions:

1. Combine the barbecue sauce mixture ingredients in a small bowl. Brush the chops with the sauce and place on a broiling rack with a pan underneath.

2. BROIL 8 minutes, turn with tongs, and broil for another 8 minutes, or until the meat is cooked to your preference.

Traditional Pot Roast

Servings: 6
Cooking Time: 75 Minutes

Ingredients:

- 2 tablespoons olive oil
- 1 teaspoon garlic powder
- 1 teaspoon fresh thyme, chopped
- ¼ teaspoon sea salt
- ¼ teaspoon freshly ground black pepper
- 1 (3-pound) beef rump roast

Directions:

1. Preheat the toaster oven to 350°F on CONVECTION BAKE for 5 minutes.

2. In a small bowl, stir the oil, garlic, thyme, salt, and pepper. Spread the mixture all over the beef.

3. Place the air-fryer basket in the baking tray and place the beef in the basket.

4. In position 1, bake for 1 hour and 15 minutes until browned and the internal temperature reaches 145°F for medium.

5. Let the roast rest 10 minutes and serve.

VEGETABLES AND VEGETARIAN

Chilaquiles

Servings: 4
Cooking Time: 25 Minutes

Ingredients:
- Oil spray (hand-pumped)
- 1¼ cups store-bought salsa
- 1 (15-ounce) can low-sodium navy or black beans, drained and rinsed
- ½ cup corn kernels
- ¼ cup chicken broth
- ¼ sweet onion, chopped
- ½ teaspoon minced garlic
- 25 tortilla chips, broken up into 2-inch pieces
- 1½ cups queso fresco cheese, crumbled
- 1 avocado, chopped
- 1 scallion, white and green parts, chopped

Directions:
1. Place the rack in position 1 and preheat the toaster oven to 400°F on BAKE for 5 minutes.
2. Lightly coat an 8-inch-square baking dish with oil spray and set aside.
3. In a large bowl, stir the salsa, beans, corn, chicken broth, onion, and garlic until well mixed.
4. Add the tortilla chips and stir to combine. It is okay if the tortilla chips break up a little.
5. Transfer the mixture to the baking dish, top with the cheese, and cover tightly with foil.
6. Bake for 20 minutes until the chips are soft, the mixture is bubbly, and then uncover and bake until the cheese is golden and melted, about 5 minutes.
7. Serve topped with the avocado and scallion.

Crispy Noodle Salad

Servings: 3
Cooking Time: 22 Minutes

Ingredients:
- 6 ounces Fresh Chinese-style stir-fry or lo mein wheat noodles
- 1½ tablespoons Cornstarch
- ¾ cup Chopped stemmed and cored red bell pepper
- 2 Medium scallion(s), trimmed and thinly sliced
- 2 teaspoons Sambal oelek or other pulpy hot red pepper sauce
- 2 teaspoons Thai sweet chili sauce or red ketchup-like chili sauce, such as Heinz
- 2 teaspoons Regular or low-sodium soy sauce or tamari sauce
- 2 teaspoons Unseasoned rice vinegar
- 1 tablespoon White or black sesame seeds

Directions:
1. Bring a large saucepan of water to a boil over high heat. Add the noodles and boil for 2 minutes. Drain in a colander set in the sink. Rinse several times with cold water, shaking the colander to drain the noodles very well. Spread the noodles out on a large cutting board and air-dry for 10 minutes.
2. Preheat the toaster oven to 400°F.
3. Toss the noodles in a bowl with the cornstarch until well coated. Spread them out across the entire air fryer oven (although they will be touching and overlapping a bit). Air-fry for 6 minutes, then turn the solid mass of noodles over as one piece. If it cracks in half or smaller pieces,

just fit these back together after turning. Continue air-frying for 6 minutes, or until golden brown and crisp.

4. As the noodles cook, stir the bell pepper, scallion(s), sambal oelek, red chili sauce, soy sauce, vinegar, and sesame seeds in a serving bowl until well combined.

5. Turn the air fryer oven of noodles out onto a cutting board and cool for a minute or two. Break the mass of noodles into individual noodles and/or small chunks and add to the dressing in the serving bowl. Toss well to serve.

Crisp Cajun Potato Wedges

Servings: 2
Cooking Time: 70 Minutes

Ingredients:
- 2 medium baking potatoes, scrubbed, halved, and cut lengthwise into ½-inch-wide wedges
- 1 tablespoon vegetable oil
- Cajun seasonings:
- ¼ teaspoon chili powder
- ⅛ teaspoon cayenne
- ⅛ teaspoon dry mustard
- ⅛ teaspoon salt
- ⅛ teaspoon cumin
- ¼ teaspoon onion powder
- ¼ teaspoon paprika

Directions:
1. Preheat the toaster oven to 450° F.
2. Soak the potato wedges in cold water for 10 minutes to crisp. Drain on paper towels. Brush with the oil.
3. Combine the Cajun seasonings in a small bowl, add the wedges, and toss to coat well. Transfer to an oiled or nonstick 8½ × 8½ × 2-inch square baking (cake) pan.

4. BAKE, covered, for 40 minutes, or until the potatoes are tender. Carefully remove the cover.
5. BROIL for 20 minutes to crisp, turning with a tongs every 5 minutes until the desired crispness is achieved.

Parmesan Asparagus

Servings: 2
Cooking Time: 5 Minutes

Ingredients:
- 1 bunch asparagus, stems trimmed
- 1 teaspoon olive oil
- salt and freshly ground black pepper
- ¼ cup coarsely grated Parmesan cheese
- ½ lemon

Directions:
1. Preheat the toaster oven to 400°F.
2. Toss the asparagus with the oil and season with salt and freshly ground black pepper.
3. Transfer the asparagus to the air fryer oven and air-fry at 400°F for 5 minutes, turn the asparagus once or twice during the cooking process.
4. When the asparagus is cooked to your liking, sprinkle the asparagus generously with the Parmesan cheese and close the air fryer oven again. Let the asparagus sit for 1 minute in the turned-off air fryer oven. Then, remove the asparagus, transfer it to a serving dish and finish with a grind of black pepper and a squeeze of lemon juice.

Blistered Tomatoes

Servings: 20
Cooking Time: 15 Minutes

Ingredients:
- 1½ pounds Cherry or grape tomatoes

- Olive oil spray
- 1½ teaspoons Balsamic vinegar
- ¼ teaspoon Table salt
- ¼ teaspoon Ground black pepper

Directions:

1. Put the pan in a drawer-style air fryer oven, or a baking tray in the lower third of a toaster oven–style air fryer oven. Place a 6-inch round cake pan in the pan or on the tray for a small batch, a 7-inch round cake pan for a medium batch, or an 8-inch round cake pan for a large one. Heat the air fryer oven to 400°F with the pan in the air fryer oven. When the machine is at temperature, keep heating the pan for 5 minutes more.

2. Place the tomatoes in a large bowl, coat them with the olive oil spray, toss gently, then spritz a couple of times more, tossing after each spritz, until the tomatoes are glistening.

3. Pour the tomatoes into the cake pan and air-fry undisturbed for 10 minutes, or until they split and begin to brown.

4. Use kitchen tongs and a nonstick-safe spatula, or silicone baking mitts, to remove the cake pan from the air fryer oven. Toss the hot tomatoes with the vinegar, salt, and pepper. Cool in the pan for a few minutes before serving.

Panzanella Salad With Crispy Croutons

Servings: 4
Cooking Time: 3 Minutes

Ingredients:

- ½ French baguette, sliced in half lengthwise
- 2 large cloves garlic
- 2 large ripe tomatoes, divided
- 2 small Persian cucumbers, quartered and diced

- ¼ cup Kalamata olives
- 1 tablespoon chopped, fresh oregano or 1 teaspoon dried oregano
- ¼ cup chopped fresh basil
- ¼ cup chopped fresh parsley
- ½ cup sliced red onion
- 2 tablespoons red wine vinegar
- ¼ cup extra-virgin olive oil
- Salt and pepper, to taste

Directions:

1. Preheat the toaster oven to 380°F.

2. Place the baguette into the air fryer oven and toast for 3 to 5 minutes or until lightly golden brown.

3. Remove the bread from air fryer oven and immediately rub 1 raw garlic clove firmly onto the inside portion of each piece of bread, scraping the garlic onto the bread.

4. Slice 1 of the tomatoes in half and rub the cut edge of one half of the tomato onto the toasted bread. Season the rubbed bread with sea salt to taste.

5. Cut the bread into cubes and place in a large bowl. Cube the remaining 1½ tomatoes and add to the bowl. Add the cucumbers, olives, oregano, basil, parsley, and onion; stir to mix. Drizzle the red wine vinegar into the bowl, and stir. Drizzle the olive oil over the top, stir, and adjust the seasonings with salt and pepper.

6. Serve immediately or allow to sit at room temperature up to 1 hour before serving.

Tandoori Cauliflower

Servings: 4
Cooking Time: 10 Minutes

Ingredients:

- ½ cup Plain full-fat yogurt (not Greek yogurt)

- 1½ teaspoons Yellow curry powder, purchased or homemade
- 1½ teaspoons Lemon juice
- ¾ teaspoon Table salt (optional)
- 4½ cups (about 1 pound 2 ounces) 2-inch cauliflower florets

Directions:

1. Preheat the toaster oven to 400°F.

2. Whisk the yogurt, curry powder, lemon juice, and salt (if using) in a large bowl until uniform. Add the florets and stir gently to coat the florets well and evenly. Even better, use your clean, dry hands to get the yogurt mixture down into all the nooks of the florets.

3. When the machine is at temperature, transfer the florets to the air fryer oven, spreading them gently into as close to one layer as you can. Air-fry for 10 minutes, tossing and rearranging the florets twice so that any covered or touching parts are exposed to the air currents, until lightly browned and tender if still a bit crunchy.

4. Pour the contents of the air fryer oven onto a wire rack. Cool for at least 5 minutes before serving, or serve at room temperature.

Air-fried Potato Salad

Servings: 4
Cooking Time: 15 Minutes

Ingredients:

- 1⅓ pounds Yellow potatoes, such as Yukon Golds, cut into ½-inch chunks
- 1 large Sweet white onion(s), such as Vidalia, chopped into ½-inch pieces
- 1 tablespoon plus 2 teaspoons Olive oil
- ¾ cup Thinly sliced celery
- 6 tablespoons Regular or low-fat mayonnaise (gluten-free, if a concern)
- 2½ tablespoons Apple cider vinegar
- 1½ teaspoons Dijon mustard (gluten-free, if a concern)
- ¾ teaspoon Table salt
- ¼ teaspoon Ground black pepper

Directions:

1. Preheat the toaster oven to 400°F.

2. Toss the potatoes, onion(s), and oil in a large bowl until the vegetables are glistening with oil.

3. When the machine is at temperature, transfer the vegetables to the air fryer oven, spreading them out into as even a layer as you can. Air-fry for 15 minutes, tossing and rearranging the vegetables every 3 minutes so that all surfaces get exposed to the air currents, until the vegetables are tender and even browned at the edges.

4. Pour the contents of the air fryer oven into a serving bowl. Cool for at least 5 minutes or up to 30 minutes. Add the celery, mayonnaise, vinegar, mustard, salt, and pepper. Stir well to coat. The potato salad can be made in advance; cover and refrigerate for up to 4 days.

Crispy Herbed Potatoes

Servings: 6
Cooking Time: 20 Minutes

Ingredients:

- 3 medium baking potatoes, washed and cubed
- ½ teaspoon dried thyme
- 1 teaspoon minced dried rosemary
- ½ teaspoon garlic powder
- 1 teaspoon sea salt
- ½ teaspoon black pepper
- 2 tablespoons extra-virgin olive oil
- ¼ cup chopped parsley

Directions:

1. Preheat the toaster oven to 390°F.

2. Pat the potatoes dry. In a large bowl, mix together the cubed potatoes, thyme, rosemary, garlic powder, sea salt, and pepper. Drizzle and toss with olive oil.

3. Pour the herbed potatoes into the air fryer oven. Air-fry for 20 minutes, stirring every 5 minutes.

4. Toss the cooked potatoes with chopped parsley and serve immediately.

5. VARY IT! Potatoes are versatile — add any spice or seasoning mixture you prefer and create your own favorite side dish.

Simply Sweet Potatoes

Servings: 2
Cooking Time: 35 Minutes

Ingredients:
- 2 medium sweet potatoes, scrubbed and slit on top
- ¼ teaspoon ground thyme per potato
- 1 tablespoon lemon juice per potato
- ½ teaspoon margarine per potato
- Salt and freshly ground black pepper

Directions:
1. Preheat the toaster oven to 425° F.
2. BAKE the potatoes on the oven rack for 35 minutes, or until tender.
3. Open the slit and fluff the sweet potato pulp with a fork. Sprinkle the pulp with equal portions of thyme, lemon juice, and margarine. Fluff again. Season with salt and pepper to taste.

Salt And Pepper Baked Potatoes

Servings: 40
Cooking Time: 4 Minutes

Ingredients:
- 1 to 2 tablespoons olive oil

- 4 medium russet potatoes (about 9 to 10 ounces each)
- salt and coarsely ground black pepper
- butter, sour cream, chopped fresh chives, scallions or bacon bits (optional)

Directions:
1. Preheat the toaster oven to 400°F.
2. Rub the olive oil all over the potatoes and season them generously with salt and coarsely ground black pepper. Pierce all sides of the potatoes several times with the tines of a fork.
3. Air-fry for 40 minutes, turning the potatoes over halfway through the cooking time.
4. Serve the potatoes, split open with butter, sour cream, fresh chives, scallions or bacon bits.

Baked Stuffed Acorn Squash

Servings: 2
Cooking Time: 25 Minutes

Ingredients:
- Stuffing:
- ¼ cup multigrain bread crumbs
- 1 tablespoon olive oil
- ¼ cup canned or frozen thawed corn
- 2 tablespoons chopped onion
- 1 teaspoon capers
- 1 teaspoon garlic powder
- Salt and freshly ground black pepper
- 1 medium acorn squash, halved and seeds scooped out

Directions:
1. Preheat the toaster oven to 400° F.
2. Combine the stuffing ingredients and season to taste. Fill the squash cavities with the mixture and place in an oiled or nonstick 8½ × 8½ × 2-inch square baking (cake) pan.
3. BAKE for 25 minutes, or until the squash is tender and the stuffing is lightly browned.

Parmesan Garlic Fries

Servings: 4

Cooking Time: 20 Minutes

Ingredients:

- 2 medium Yukon gold potatoes, washed
- 1 tablespoon extra-virgin olive oil
- 1 garlic clove, minced
- 2 tablespoons finely grated parmesan cheese
- ¼ teaspoon black pepper
- ¼ teaspoon salt
- 1 tablespoon freshly chopped parsley

Directions:

1. Preheat the toaster oven to 400°F.
2. Slice the potatoes into long strips about ¼-inch thick. In a large bowl, toss the potatoes with the olive oil, garlic, cheese, pepper, and salt.
3. Place the fries into the air fryer oven and air-fry for 8 minutes.
4. Remove and serve warm.

Home Fries

Servings: 4

Cooking Time: 20 Minutes

Ingredients:

- 3 pounds potatoes, cut into 1-inch cubes
- ½ teaspoon oil
- salt and pepper

Directions:

1. In a large bowl, mix the potatoes and oil thoroughly.
2. Air-fry at 390°F for 10 minutes and redistribute potatoes.
3. Air-fry for an additional 10 minutes, until brown and crisp.
4. Season with salt and pepper to taste.

Baked Mac And Cheese

Servings: 4

Cooking Time: 45 Minutes

Ingredients:

- Oil spray (hand-pumped)
- 1½ cups whole milk, room temperature
- ½ cup heavy (whipping) cream, room temperature
- 1 cup shredded cheddar cheese
- 4 ounces cream cheese, room temperature
- ½ teaspoon dry mustard
- ⅛ teaspoon sea salt
- ⅛ teaspoon freshly ground black pepper
- 1¼ cups dried elbow macaroni
- ¼ cup bread crumbs
- 2 tablespoons grated Parmesan cheese
- 1 tablespoon salted butter, melted

Directions:

1. Place the rack in position 1 and preheat the toaster oven to 375°F on CONVECTION BAKE for 5 minutes.
2. Lightly coat an 8-inch-square baking dish with the oil spray.
3. In a large bowl, stir the milk, cream, cheddar, cream cheese, mustard, salt, and pepper until well combined.
4. Transfer the mixture to the baking dish, stir in the macaroni and cover tightly with foil.
5. Bake for 35 minutes.
6. While the macaroni is baking, in a small bowl, stir the bread crumbs, Parmesan, and butter to form coarse crumbs. Set aside.
7. Take the baking dish out of the oven, uncover, stir, and evenly cover with the bread crumb mixture.
8. Bake uncovered for an additional 10 minutes until the pasta is tender, bubbly, and golden brown. Serve.

Asparagus Ronald

Servings: 4
Cooking Time: 25 Minutes

Ingredients:

- 20 asparagus spears, rinsed and hard stem ends cut off
- 1 tablespoon soy sauce
- 3 tablespoons lemon juice
- 3 tablespoons olive oil
- Salt and freshly ground black pepper
- 3 tablespoons crumbled feta cheese

Directions:

1. Preheat the toaster oven to 400° F.
2. Place the asparagus spears in a 1-quart 8½ × 8½ × 4-inch ovenproof baking dish.
3. Drizzle the soy sauce, lemon juice, and olive oil over the asparagus spears. Season to taste with salt and pepper. Cover the dish with aluminum foil.
4. BAKE for 25 minutes, or until tender. Sprinkle with the feta cheese before serving.

Baked Stuffed Potatoes With Vegetables

Servings: 2
Cooking Time: 30 Minutes

Ingredients:

- 2 large baking potatoes, baked, cooled, and pulp scooped out to make shells
- Stuffing:
- 1 carrot, shredded
- ½ bell pepper, seeded and shredded
- 2 tablespoons broccoli, shredded
- 2 tablespoons cauliflower, shredded
- 3 tablespoons fat-free half-and-half
- 1 teaspoon paprika

- ½ teaspoon garlic powder
- ½ teaspoon caraway seeds
- Salt and butcher's pepper to taste

Directions:

1. Preheat the toaster oven to 400° F.
2. Combine the stuffing mixture ingredients, mixing well. Fill the potato shells with the mixture and place the shells in an oiled 8½ × 8½ × 2-inch square baking (cake) pan.
3. BAKE for 25 minutes or until vegetables are cooked.
4. BROIL for 5 minutes, or until the tops are lightly browned.

Street Corn

Servings: 4
Cooking Time: 10 Minutes

Ingredients:

- 1 tablespoon butter
- 4 ears corn
- ⅓ cup plain Greek yogurt
- 2 tablespoons Parmesan cheese
- ½ teaspoon paprika
- ½ teaspoon garlic powder
- ¼ teaspoon salt
- ¼ teaspoon black pepper
- ¼ cup finely chopped cilantro

Directions:

1. Preheat the toaster oven to 400°F.
2. In a medium microwave-safe bowl, melt the butter in the microwave. Lightly brush the outside of the ears of corn with the melted butter.
3. Place the corn into the air fryer oven and air-fry for 5 minutes, flip the corn, and cook another 5 minutes.

4. Meanwhile, in a medium bowl, mix the yogurt, cheese, paprika, garlic powder, salt, and pepper. Set aside.

5. Carefully remove the corn from the air fryer oven and let cool 3 minutes. Brush the outside edges with the yogurt mixture and top with fresh chopped cilantro. Serve immediately.

Rosemary New Potatoes

Servings: 4
Cooking Time: 6 Minutes

Ingredients:

* 3 large red potatoes (enough to make 3 cups sliced)
* ¼ teaspoon ground rosemary
* ¼ teaspoon ground thyme
* ⅛ teaspoon salt
* ⅛ teaspoon ground black pepper
* 2 teaspoons extra-light olive oil

Directions:

1. Preheat the toaster oven to 330°F.
2. Place potatoes in large bowl and sprinkle with rosemary, thyme, salt, and pepper.
3. Stir with a spoon to distribute seasonings evenly.
4. Add oil to potatoes and stir again to coat well.
5. Air-fry at 330°F for 4 minutes. Stir and break apart any that have stuck together.
6. Cook an additional 2 minutes or until fork-tender.

Brussels Sprout And Ham Salad

Servings: 3
Cooking Time: 12 Minutes

Ingredients:

* 1 pound 2-inch-in-length Brussels sprouts, quartered through the stem
* 6 ounces Smoked ham steak, any rind removed, diced (gluten-free, if a concern)
* ¼ teaspoon Caraway seeds
* Vegetable oil spray
* ¼ cup Brine from a jar of pickles (gluten-free if a concern)
* ¾ teaspoon Ground black pepper

Directions:

1. Preheat the toaster oven to 375°F .
2. Toss the Brussels sprout quarters, ham, and caraway seeds in a bowl until well combined. Generously coat the top of the mixture with vegetable oil spray, toss again, spray again, and repeat a couple of times until the vegetables and ham are glistening.
3. When the machine is at temperature, scrape the contents of the bowl into the air fryer oven, spreading it into as close to one layer as you can. Air-fry for 12 minutes, tossing and rearranging the pieces at least twice so that any covered or touching parts are eventually exposed to the air currents, until the Brussels sprouts are tender and a little brown at the edges.
4. Dump the contents of the air fryer oven into a serving bowl. Scrape any caraway seeds from the bottom of the air fryer oven or the tray under the pan attachment into the bowl as well. Add the pickle brine and pepper. Toss well to coat. Serve warm.

Stuffed Onions

Servings: 6
Cooking Time: 27 Minutes

Ingredients:

* 6 Small 3½- to 4-ounce yellow or white onions
* Olive oil spray

- 6 ounces Bulk sweet Italian sausage meat (gluten-free, if a concern)
- 9 Cherry tomatoes, chopped
- 3 tablespoons Seasoned Italian-style dried bread crumbs (gluten-free, if a concern)
- 3 tablespoons (about ½ ounce) Finely grated Parmesan cheese

Directions:

1. Preheat the toaster oven to 325°F (or 330°F, if that's the closest setting).

2. Cut just enough off the root ends of the onions so they will stand up on a cutting board when this end is turned down. Carefully peel off just the brown, papery skin. Now cut the top quarter off each and place the onion back on the cutting board with this end facing up. Use a flatware spoon (preferably a serrated grapefruit spoon) or a melon baller to scoop out the "insides" (interior layers) of the onion, leaving enough of the bottom and side walls so that the onion does not collapse. Depending on the thickness of the layers in the onion, this may be one or two of those layers—or even three, if they're very thin.

3. Coat the insides and outsides of the onions with olive oil spray. Set the onion "shells" in the air fryer oven and air-fry for 15 minutes.

4. Meanwhile, make the filling. Set a medium skillet over medium heat for a couple of minutes, then crumble in the sausage meat. Cook, stirring often, until browned, about 4 minutes. Transfer the contents of the skillet to a medium bowl (leave the fat behind in the skillet or add it to the bowl, depending on your cross-trainer regimen). Stir in the tomatoes, bread crumbs, and cheese until well combined.

5. When the onions are ready, use a nonstick-safe spatula to gently transfer them to a cutting board. Increase the air fryer oven's temperature to 350°F .

6. Pack the sausage mixture into the onion shells, gently compacting the filling and mounding it up at the top.

7. When the machine is at temperature, set the onions stuffing side up in the air fryer oven with at least ¼ inch between them. Air-fry for 12 minutes, or until lightly browned and sizzling hot.

8. Use a nonstick-safe spatula, and perhaps a flatware fork for balance, to transfer the onions to a cutting board or serving platter. Cool for 5 minutes before serving.

Quick Broccoli Quiche

Servings: 6
Cooking Time: 35 Minutes

Ingredients:
- 12 sheets phyllo dough
- Olive oil for brushing phyllo sheets
- Filling:
- ½ cup chopped fresh broccoli or ½ cup frozen chopped broccoli, thawed and well drained
- 4 eggs, well beaten
- 2 tablespoons fat-free half-and-half
- 3 tablespoons nonfat plain yogurt
- ½ cup low-fat ricotta cheese
- 3 tablespoons finely chopped onion
- Salt and freshly ground pepper
- ¼ cup shredded part-skim mozzarella cheese

Directions:

1. Preheat the toaster oven to 300° F.

2. Layer the phyllo sheets in an oiled or nonstick 9¾-inch-diameter pie pan, brushing each sheet with olive oil and folding it to fit the pan. Bake for 5 minutes, or until lightly browned. Remove from the oven and set aside.

3. Mix together all the filling ingredients in a medium bowl and season to taste with salt and pepper. Pour the mixture into the phyllo dough crust and sprinkle with the mozzarella cheese.

4. BAKE at 400° F. for 30 minutes, or until the surface is springy to touch and browned.

Molasses Baked Beans

Servings: 4
Cooking Time: 60 Minutes

Ingredients:
- Oil spray (hand-pumped)
- 3 (15-ounce) cans low-sodium canned pinto beans, drained and rinsed
- ½ sweet onion, chopped
- ½ cup low-sodium vegetable broth
- ½ cup tomato paste
- ¼ cup blackstrap molasses
- 1 tablespoon stone-ground mustard
- 1 teaspoon garlic powder

Directions:
1. Place the rack on position 1 and preheat the toaster oven on BAKE to 350°F for 5 minutes.

2. Lightly coat a 1½-quart casserole dish with oil spray.

3. In the dish, combine the beans, onion, broth, tomato paste, molasses, mustard, and garlic powder.

4. Cover the dish with a lid or foil and bake until very tender and the sauce is thick, about 1 hour. Serve.

Roasted Cauliflower With Garlic And Capers

Servings: 3
Cooking Time: 10 Minutes

Ingredients:
- 3 cups (about 15 ounces) 1-inch cauliflower florets
- 2 tablespoons Olive oil
- 1½ tablespoons Drained and rinsed capers, chopped
- 2 teaspoons Minced garlic
- ¼ teaspoon Table salt
- Up to ¼ teaspoon Red pepper flakes

Directions:
1. Preheat the toaster oven to 375°F .

2. Stir the cauliflower florets, olive oil, capers, garlic, salt, and red pepper flakes in a large bowl until the florets are evenly coated.

3. When the machine is at temperature, put the florets in the pan, spreading them out to as close to one layer as you can. Air-fry for 10 minutes, tossing once to get any covered pieces exposed to the air currents, until tender and lightly browned.

4. Dump the contents of the air fryer oven into a serving bowl or onto a serving platter. Cool for a minute or two before serving.

Pecan Parmesan Cauliflower

Servings: 4
Cooking Time: 35 Minutes

Ingredients:
- 2½ cups (frozen thawed or fresh) thinly sliced cauliflower florets
- Salt and freshly ground black pepper
- 3 tablespoons freshly grated Parmesan cheese
- ½ cup ground pecans

Directions:
1. Preheat the toaster oven to 400° F.

2. Combine the florets and oil in a 1-quart 8½ × 8½ × 4-inch ovenproof baking dish, tossing to

coat well. Season to taste with salt and pepper. Cover the dish with aluminum foil.

3. BAKE for 25 minutes, or until tender. Uncover and sprinkle with the cheese and pecans.

4. BROIL for 10 minutes, or until lightly browned.

Grits Again

Servings: 2
Cooking Time: 10 Minutes

Ingredients:

- cooked grits
- plain breadcrumbs
- oil for misting or cooking spray
- honey or maple syrup for serving (optional)

Directions:

1. While grits are still warm, spread them into a square or rectangular baking pan, about ½-inch thick. If your grits are thicker than that, scoop some out into another pan.

2. Chill several hours or overnight, until grits are cold and firm.

3. When ready to cook, pour off any water that has collected in pan and cut grits into 2- to 3-inch squares.

4. Dip grits squares in breadcrumbs and place in air fryer oven in single layer, close but not touching.

5. Air-fry at 390°F for 10 minutes, until heated through and crispy brown on the outside.

6. Serve while hot either plain or with a drizzle of honey or maple syrup.

Roasted Eggplant Halves With Herbed Ricotta

Servings: 3
Cooking Time: 20 Minutes

Ingredients:

- 3 5- to 6-ounce small eggplants, stemmed
- Olive oil spray
- ¼ teaspoon Table salt
- ¼ teaspoon Ground black pepper
- ½ cup Regular or low-fat ricotta
- 1½ tablespoons Minced fresh basil leaves
- 1¼ teaspoons Minced fresh oregano leaves
- Honey

Directions:

1. Preheat the toaster oven to 325°F (or 330°F, if that's the closest setting).

2. Cut the eggplants in half lengthwise. Set them cut side up on your work surface. Using the tip of a paring knife, make a series of slits about three-quarters down into the flesh of each eggplant half; work at a 45-degree angle to the (former) stem across the vegetable and make the slits about ½ inch apart. Make a second set of equidistant slits at a 90-degree angle to the first slits, thus creating a crosshatch pattern in the vegetable.

3. Generously coat the cut sides of the eggplants with olive oil spray. Sprinkle the salt and pepper over the cut surfaces.

4. Set the eggplant halves cut side up in the air fryer oven with as much air space between them as possible. Air-fry undisturbed for 20 minutes, or until soft and golden.

5. Use kitchen tongs to gently transfer the eggplant halves to serving plates or a platter. Cool for 5 minutes.

6. Whisk the ricotta, basil, and oregano in a small bowl until well combined. Top the eggplant halves with this mixture. Drizzle the halves with honey to taste before serving warm.

Potato Skins

Servings: 4
Cooking Time: 20 Minutes

Ingredients:

- 4 potato shells

Directions:

1. Place 4 potato shells in an oiled or nonstick 8½ × 8½ × 2-inch square baking (cake) pan.

2. Brush, sprinkle, and fill with a variety of seasonings or ingredients.

3. BROIL 20 minutes, or until browned and crisped to your preference.

DESSERTS

Goat Cheese–stuffed Nectarines

Servings: 4
Cooking Time: 10 Minutes

Ingredients:
- 4 ripe nectarines, halved and pitted
- 1 tablespoon olive oil
- 1 cup soft goat cheese, room temperature
- 1 tablespoon maple syrup
- ¼ teaspoon vanilla extract
- ¼ teaspoon ground cinnamon
- 2 tablespoons pecans, chopped

Directions:
1. Preheat the toaster oven to 350°F on AIR FRY for 5 minutes.
2. Place the air-fryer basket in the baking tray and place the nectarines in the basket, hollow-side up. Brush the tops and hollow of the fruit with the olive oil.
3. In position 2, air fry for 5 minutes to soften and lightly brown the fruit.
4. While the fruit is air frying, in a small bowl, stir the goat cheese, maple syrup, vanilla, and cinnamon until well blended.
5. Take the fruit out and evenly divide the cheese filling between the halves. Air fry for 5 minutes until the filling is heated through and a little melted.
6. Serve topped with pecans.

Apricot Coffee Cake

Servings: 1
Cooking Time: 15 Minutes

Ingredients:
- 2 cups baking mix
- 3 ounces cream cheese
- ¼ cup unsalted butter
- ½ cup chopped pecans, toasted
- ⅓ cup whole milk
- ¾ cup apricot preserves
- GLAZE
- 1 cup confectioners' sugar
- ¼ teaspoon almond extract
- 1 to 2 tablespoons whole milk

Directions:
1. Preheat the toaster oven to 425 °F. Grease a 12 x 12-inch baking pan.
2. Place the baking mix in a large bowl. Using a pastry cutter or two knives, cut the cream cheese and butter into the baking mix until the mixture is crumbly throughout. Add the pecans and milk and mix well.
3. Turn the dough onto a lightly floured surface and knead lightly about 8 times. Roll the dough into a 12 x 8-inch rectangle. Place the rolled dough diagonally on the prepared pan. Spread the preserves lengthwise down the center of the dough. Make 2 ½-inch cuts at 1-inch intervals on both sides of the filling. Fold the strips over the preserves, overlapping in the center. Bake for 15 minutes or until golden brown.
4. Make the Glaze: Whisk the confectioners' sugar, almond extract, and 1 tablespoon milk in a small bowl until smooth. Add additional milk, as needed, to make a glaze consistency.
5. Drizzle the glaze over the warm coffee cake.

Blueberry Cookies

Servings: 4
Cooking Time: 12 Minutes

Ingredients:

- 1 egg
- 1 tablespoon margarine, at room temperature
- ⅓ cup sugar
- 1¼ cups unbleached flour
- Salt to taste
- 1 teaspoon baking powder
- 1 10-ounce package frozen blueberries, well drained, or
- 1½ cups fresh blueberries, rinsed and drained

Directions:

1. Preheat the toaster oven to 400° F.
2. Beat together the egg, margarine, and sugar in a medium bowl with an electric mixer until smooth. Add the flour, salt, and baking powder, mixing thoroughly. Gently stir in the blueberries just to blend. Do not overmix.
3. Drop by teaspoonfuls on an oiled or nonstick 6½ × 10-inch baking sheet or an oiled or nonstick 8½ × 8½ × 2-inch square baking (cake) pan.
4. BAKE for 12 minutes, or until the cookies are golden brown.

Coconut Rice Pudding

Servings: 6
Cooking Time: 55 Minutes

Ingredients:

- ½ cup short-grain brown rice
- Pudding mixture:
- 1 egg, beaten
- 1 tablespoon cornstarch
- ½ cup fat-free half-and-half
- ½ cup chopped raisins
- 1 teaspoon vanilla extract
- ½ teaspoon ground cinnamon
- ½ teaspoon grated nutmeg
- Salt to taste
- ¼ cup shredded sweetened coconut
- Fat-free whipped topping

Directions:

1. Preheat the toaster oven to 400° F.
2. Combine the rice and 1½ cups water in a 1-quart 8½ × 8½ × 4-inch ovenproof baking dish. Cover with aluminum foil.
3. BAKE, covered, for 45 minutes, or until the rice is tender. Remove from the oven and add the pudding mixture ingredients, mixing well.
4. BAKE, uncovered, for 10 minutes, or until the top is lightly browned. Sprinkle the top with coconut and chill before serving. Top with fat-free whipped topping.

Cowboy Cookies

Servings: 3
Cooking Time: 14 Minutes

Ingredients:

- Recommended Hamilton Beach® Product: Stand Mixers
- 1 cup butter
- 1 cup sugar
- 1 cup light brown sugar
- 2 eggs
- 2 cups flour
- 1 teaspoon baking soda
- ½ teaspoon baking powder
- ½ teaspoon salt
- 2 cups oatmeal
- 1 tablespoon vanilla
- 12 ounces chocolate chips
- 1 ½ cups coconut

Directions:

1. Preheat the toaster oven to 350°F.

2. With flat beater attachment, cream together butter, sugar, and brown sugar at a medium setting until well blended. Mix in vanilla and eggs. Reduce speed and gradually add flour, baking soda, baking powder, and salt mix until smooth.

3. On a low setting, mix in oatmeal, chocolate chips, and coconut until well mixed. Drop rounded spoon full onto ungreased cookie sheet.

4. Bake on middle rack of oven for 12 to 14 minutes.

Graham Cracker Crust

Servings: 4
Cooking Time: 14 Minutes

Ingredients:

- 1⅓ cups reduced-fat graham cracker crumbs
- 2 tablespoons brown sugar
- 1 teaspoon ground cinnamon
- Salt to taste
- 1 tablespoon margarine
- 2 tablespoons vegetable oil

Directions:

1. Process the graham crackers in a food processor or blender to produce finely ground crumbs. Add the sugar, cinnamon, and salt and blend by stirring. Set aside.

2. Heat the margarine and oil under a broiler for 4 minutes, or until the margarine is almost melted. Remove from the oven and stir until the margarine is completely melted. Add the graham cracker crumbs and mix thoroughly.

3. Press the mixture into a 9¾-inch pie pan, spreading it out evenly from the middle and up the sides of the pan.

4. BAKE at 350° F. for 10 minutes, or until lightly browned. Cool before filling.

Heritage Chocolate Chip Cookies

Servings: 16-18
Cooking Time: 12 Minutes

Ingredients:

- 1 1/2 cups all-purpose flour
- 1 teaspoon baking powder
- 1/2 teaspoon salt
- 1 large egg, unbeaten
- 1/2 cup shortening
- 1/2 cup packed dark brown sugar
- 1/4 cup granulated sugar
- 2 teaspoons vanilla extract
- 1 tablespoon milk
- 1 cup chocolate chips

Directions:

1. Preheat the toaster oven to 375ºF.

2. Place all ingredients except chocolate chips in large mixer bowl. With electric mixer on low speed, beat until ingredients are mixed. Gradually increase speed to medium and beat 3 minutes, stopping to scrape bowl as needed.

3. Add chocolate chips and beat on low until blended.

4. Line cookie sheets with parchment paper. Using a small scoop, place 12 scoops of cookie dough about 1-inch apart on parchment.

5. Bake 10 to 12 minutes or until cookies are browned. Slide parchment with baked cookies onto rack to cool. Repeat with remaining dough.

Hasselback Apple Crisp

Servings: 4

Cooking Time: 20 Minutes

Ingredients:

- 2 large Gala apples, peeled, cored and cut in half
- ¼ cup butter, melted
- ½ teaspoon ground cinnamon
- 2 tablespoons sugar
- Topping
- 3 tablespoons butter, melted
- 2 tablespoons brown sugar
- ¼ cup chopped pecans
- 2 tablespoons rolled oats
- 1 tablespoon flour
- vanilla ice cream
- caramel sauce

Directions:

1. Place the apples cut side down on a cutting board. Slicing from stem end to blossom end, make 8 to 10 slits down the apple halves but only slice three quarters of the way through the apple, not all the way through to the cutting board.

2. Preheat the toaster oven to 330°F and pour a little water into the bottom of the air fryer oven drawer. (This will help prevent the grease that drips into the bottom drawer from burning and smoking.)

3. Transfer the apples to the air fryer oven, flat side down. Combine ¼ cup of melted butter, cinnamon and sugar in a small bowl. Brush this butter mixture onto the apples and air-fry at 330°F for 15 minutes. Baste the apples several times with the butter mixture during the cooking process.

4. While the apples are air-frying, make the filling. Combine 3 tablespoons of melted butter with the brown sugar, pecans, rolled oats and flour in a bowl. Stir with a fork until the mixture resembles small crumbles.

5. When the timer on the air fryer oven is up spoon the topping down the center of the apples. Air-fry at 330°F for an additional 5 minutes.

6. Transfer the apples to a serving plate and serve with vanilla ice cream and caramel sauce.

Easy Peach Turnovers

Servings: 6

Cooking Time: 35 Minutes

Ingredients:

- 1 ½ tablespoons granulated sugar
- 1 teaspoon cornstarch
- ¾ cup chopped peeled peaches, fresh or frozen and thawed
- ½ teaspoon grated lemon zest
- ⅛ teaspoon ground nutmeg
- Dash table salt
- 1 sheet frozen puff pastry, about 9 inches square, thawed (½ of a 17.3-ounce package)
- 1 large egg
- Coarse white sugar
- GLAZE
- ¾ cup confectioners' sugar
- ½ teaspoon pure vanilla extract
- 1 to 2 tablespoons milk

Directions:

1. Line a 12 x 12-inch baking pan with parchment paper.

2. Stir the granulated sugar and cornstarch in a medium bowl. Stir in the peaches, lemon zest, nutmeg, and salt. Mix until the sugar-cornstarch mixture coats the peaches evenly and the sugar begins to dissolve; set aside.

3. On a lightly floured board, roll the puff pastry sheet into a 13 ½ x 9-inch rectangle. Cut the puff pastry into 6 (4 ½-inch) squares. Lightly beat the egg in a small bowl, then brush the edges of each puff pastry square with the egg. Reserve the remaining egg to brush on top of each turnover.

4. Spoon about 2 tablespoons peach mixture into the center of each square. Fold the pastry over the peaches to form a triangle, pinching to seal the edges. Using the tines of a fork, crimp the edges tightly. Lightly brush the top of each turnover with the egg. Sprinkle each with the coarse sugar.

5. Place the turnovers on the prepared pan. Freeze the turnovers for 15 minutes.

6. Preheat the toaster oven to 375°F. Bake for 15 to 20 minutes or until golden brown. Let cool 5 to 10 minutes.

7. Meanwhile make the glaze: Whisk the confectioners' sugar, vanilla, and 1 tablespoon milk in a small bowl until smooth. If needed, stir in the additional milk to reach the desired consistency. Drizzle the glaze from the tip of a teaspoon in decorative stripes over the turnovers.

Glazed Apple Crostata

Servings: 6
Cooking Time: 35 Minutes

Ingredients:
- PASTRY
- 1 ¼ cups all-purpose flour
- 3 tablespoons granulated sugar
- ¼ teaspoon table salt
- ½ cup unsalted butter, cut into 1-inch pieces
- 2 ½ to 3 ½ tablespoons ice water
- FILLING
- ¼ cup granulated sugar
- 3 tablespoons all-purpose flour
- ½ teaspoon ground cinnamon
- ¼ teaspoon ground nutmeg
- Dash table salt
- 3 large Granny Smith apples, peeled, cored, and thinly sliced
- 1 tablespoon unsalted butter, cut into small pieces
- 1 large egg
- Coarse white sugar
- GLAZE
- ¼ cup apricot preserves or apple jelly

Directions:

1. Place the flour, sugar, and salt in the work bowl of a food processor. Pulse to combine. Add the butter and pulse until it forms coarse crumbs. With the motor running, drizzle in enough cold water that the mixture comes together and forms a dough. Shape the dough into a disk, wrap in plastic wrap, and refrigerate for at least 1 hour or until chilled.

2. Make the filling: Stir the sugar, flour, cinnamon, nutmeg, and salt in a large bowl. Add the apples and stir to coat; set aside.

3. Preheat the toaster oven to 400°F. Line a 12-inch pizza pan or 12 x 12-inch baking pan with parchment paper.

4. Roll the pastry into a 12-inch circle on a lightly floured board. Gently fold the dough into quarters and transfer to the prepared pan. Unfold the dough. Pile the filling in the center of the pastry, leaving a 1- to 2-inch border around the edges. Dot the apples with the butter. Fold the edges of the crust up around the outer edge of the apples. Whisk the egg in a small bowl, then brush the edges of the crust with the egg. Sprinkle the crust with coarse sugar.

5. Bake for 30 to 35 minutes or until golden brown and the apples are tender.

6. Set on a wire rack. For the glaze, microwave the preserves in a small, microwave-safe glass bowl on High (100 percent) power for 30 seconds or until melted. Pour the preserves through a fine mesh strainer. Brush the warm preserves over the apples (but not over the crust). Serve warm.

Freezer-to-oven Chocolate Chip Cookies

Servings: 6
Cooking Time: 15 Minutes

Ingredients:

- 2 ½ cups all-purpose flour
- 1 teaspoon baking soda
- ½ teaspoon table salt
- ¼ teaspoon baking powder
- 1 cup unsalted butter, softened
- 1 cup packed dark brown sugar
- ¾ cup granulated sugar
- 2 large eggs
- 2 teaspoons pure vanilla extract
- 1 (12-ounce) package semisweet chocolate chips

Directions:

1. Preheat the toaster oven to 375°F. Line a 12 x 12-inch baking sheet with parchment paper.

2. Whisk the flour, baking soda, salt, and baking powder in a medium bowl; set aside.

3. Beat the butter, brown sugar, and granulated sugar in a large bowl with a handheld mixer at medium-high speed for 2 minutes or until creamy. Beat in the eggs, one at a time, beating well after each addition. Beat in the vanilla. Mix in the dry ingredients until blended. Stir in the chocolate chips.

4. Using a 2-tablespoon scoop, shape the batter into balls about 1 ½ inches in diameter. Arrange the cookies 1 inch apart on the prepared baking sheet. Bake for 13 to 15 minutes or until golden brown. Remove from the oven and let cool for 1 minute, then transfer the cookies to a wire rack.

Easy Churros

Servings: 12
Cooking Time: 10 Minutes

Ingredients:

- ½ cup Water
- 4 tablespoons (¼ cup/½ stick) Butter
- ¼ teaspoon Table salt
- ½ cup All-purpose flour
- 2 Large egg(s)
- ¼ cup Granulated white sugar
- 2 teaspoons Ground cinnamon

Directions:

1. Bring the water, butter, and salt to a boil in a small saucepan set over high heat, stirring occasionally.

2. When the butter has fully melted, reduce the heat to medium and stir in the flour to form a dough. Continue cooking, stirring constantly, to dry out the dough until it coats the bottom and sides of the pan with a film, even a crust. Remove the pan from the heat, scrape the dough into a bowl, and cool for 15 minutes.

3. Using an electric hand mixer at medium speed, beat in the egg, or eggs one at a time, until the dough is smooth and firm enough to hold its shape.

4. Mix the sugar and cinnamon in a small bowl. Scoop up 1 tablespoon of the dough and roll it in the sugar mixture to form a small, coated tube about ½ inch in diameter and 2 inches long. Set it

aside and make 5 more tubes for the small batch or 11 more for the large one.

5. Set the tubes on a plate and freeze for 20 minutes. Meanwhile, preheat the toaster oven to 375°F.

6. Set 3 frozen tubes in the air fryer oven for a small batch or 6 for a large one with as much air space between them as possible. Air-fry undisturbed for 10 minutes, or until puffed, brown, and set.

7. Use kitchen tongs to transfer the churros to a wire rack to cool for at least 5 minutes. Meanwhile, air-fry and cool the second batch of churros in the same way.

Lemon Torte

Servings: 6
Cooking Time: 16 Minutes

Ingredients:

- First mixture:
- ¼ cup margarine, at room temperature
- ½ teaspoon grated lemon zest
- 3 egg yolks
- ¼ cup sugar
- ⅓ cup unbleached flour
- 3 tablespoons cornstarch
- Second mixture:
- 3 egg whites
- 2 tablespoons sugar
- Cream Cheese Frosting (recipe follows)

Directions:

1. Beat together the first mixture ingredients in a medium bowl with an electric mixer until the mixture is smooth. Set aside. Clean the electric mixer beaters.

2. Beat the second mixture together: Beat the egg whites into soft peaks in a medium bowl,

gradually adding the sugar, and continue beating until the peaks are stiff. Fold the first mixture into the second mixture to make the torte batter.

3. Pour ½ cup torte batter into a small oiled or nonstick 3½ × 7½ × 2¼-inch loaf pan.

4. BROIL for 1 or 2 minutes, or until lightly browned. Remove from the oven.

5. Pour and spread evenly another ½ cup batter on top of the first layer. Broil again for 1 or 2 minutes, or until lightly browned. Repeat the process until all the batter is used up. When cool, run a knife around the sides to loosen and invert onto a plate. Chill. Frost with Cream Cheese Frosting and serve chilled.

Chocolate Caramel Pecan Cupcakes

Servings: 6
Cooking Time: 20 Minutes

Ingredients:

- 6 tablespoons all-purpose flour
- 6 tablespoons unsweetened cocoa powder
- ¼ teaspoon baking soda
- ¼ teaspoon baking powder
- ⅛ teaspoon table salt
- 6 tablespoons unsalted butter, softened
- ½ cup granulated sugar
- 1 large egg
- ½ teaspoon pure vanilla extract
- ½ cup sour cream
- BUTTERCREAM FROSTING
- ¼ cup unsalted butter, softened
- 1 ¾ cups confectioners' sugar
- 2 to 3 tablespoons half-and-half or milk
- 1 teaspoon pure vanilla extract
- Caramel ice cream topping
- ¼ cup caramelized chopped pecans

Directions:

1. Preheat the toaster oven to 350°F. Line a 6-cup muffin pan with cupcake papers.

2. Whisk the flour, cocoa, baking soda, baking powder, and salt in a small bowl; set aside.

3. Beat the butter and granulated sugar in a large bowl with a handheld mixer at medium-high speed for 2 minutes, or until the mixture is light and creamy. Beat in the egg well. Beat in the vanilla.

4. On low speed, beat in the flour mixture in thirds, alternating with the sour cream, beginning and ending with the flour mixture. The batter will be thick.

5. Spoon the batter evenly into the prepared cupcake cups, filling each about three-quarters full. Bake for 18 to 20 minutes, or until a wooden pick inserted into the center comes out clean. Place on a wire rack and let cool completely.

6. Meanwhile, make the frosting: Beat the butter in a large bowl using a handheld mixer on medium-high speed until creamy. Gradually beat in the confectioners' sugar. Beat in 2 tablespoons of half-and-half and the vanilla. Beat in the remaining tablespoon of half-and-half, as needed, until the frosting is of desired consistency.

7. Frost each cooled cupcake. Drizzle the caramel topping in thin, decorative stripes over the frosting. Top with the caramelized pecans.

Soft Peanut Butter Cookies

Servings: 12
Cooking Time: 20 Minutes

Ingredients:
- 1/2 cup vegetable shortening
- 1/2 cup peanut butter
- 1 1/4 cups light brown sugar
- 1 egg
- 1 teaspoon vanilla
- 1/2 teaspoon salt
- 1 1/2 cups flour
- 1 teaspoon baking soda
- Sugar crystals

Directions:

1. Preheat the toaster oven to 275°F.

2. Using the flat beater attachment, beat shortening, peanut butter, brown sugar, egg, and vanilla at a medium setting until well blended.

3. Reduce speed to low and gradually add dry ingredients until blended. Dough will be crumbly.

4. Roll 3 tablespoon-size portions of the dough into a ball. Place on ungreased cookie sheet.

5. Press to 1/2-inch thick. Sprinkle with sugar crystals.

6. Bake 18 to 20 minutes. Do not overcook.

Little Swedish Coffee Cakes

Servings: 4
Cooking Time: 30 Minutes

Ingredients:
- Cake batter:
- 1 cup unbleached flour
- 1 teaspoon baking powder
- ½ cup sugar
- ½ cup finely ground pecans
- ¾ cup low-fat buttermilk
- 1 tablespoon vegetable oil
- 1 egg, lightly beaten
- 1 teaspoon vanilla extract
- Salt to taste
- Sifted confectioners' sugar
- Canola oil for brushing pan

Directions:

1. Preheat the toaster oven to 350° F.

2. Combine the cake batter ingredients in a bowl, mixing well. Pour the batter into an oiled or nonstick 8½ × 8½ × 2-inch square baking (cake) pan.

3. BAKE for 30 minutes, or until a toothpick inserted in the center comes out clean. Run a knife around the edge of the pan, invert, and place on a rack to cool. Sprinkle the top with sifted confectioners' sugar and cut into small squares.

Brown Sugar Baked Apples

Servings: 4
Cooking Time: 15 Minutes

Ingredients:
- 3 Small tart apples, preferably McIntosh
- 4 tablespoons (¼ cup/½ stick) Butter
- 6 tablespoons Light brown sugar
- Ground cinnamon
- Table salt

Directions:
1. Preheat the toaster oven to 400°F.

2. Stem the apples, then cut them in half through their "equators" (that is, not the stem ends). Use a melon baller to core the apples, taking care not to break through the flesh and skin at any point but creating a little well in the center of each half.

3. When the machine is at temperature, remove the baking pan and set it on a heat-safe work surface. Set the apple halves cut side up in the baking pan with as much air space between them as possible. Even a fraction of an inch will work. Drop 2 teaspoons of butter into the well in the center of each apple half. Sprinkle each half with 1 tablespoon brown sugar and a pinch each ground cinnamon and table salt.

4. Return the baking pan to the machine. Air-fry undisturbed for 15 minutes, or until the apple halves have softened and the brown sugar has caramelized.

5. Use a nonstick-safe spatula to transfer the apple halves cut side up to a wire rack. Cool for at least 10 minutes before serving, or serve at room temperature.

Individual Peach Crisps

Servings: 2
Cooking Time: 60 Minutes

Ingredients:
- 2 tablespoons granulated sugar, divided
- 1 teaspoon lemon juice
- ¼ teaspoon cornstarch
- ⅛ teaspoon table salt, divided
- 1 pound frozen sliced peaches, thawed
- ⅓ cup whole almonds or pecans, chopped fine
- ¼ cup (1¼ ounces) all-purpose flour
- 2 tablespoons packed light brown sugar
- ⅛ teaspoon ground cinnamon
- Pinch ground nutmeg
- 3 tablespoons unsalted butter, melted and cooled

Directions:
1. Adjust toaster oven rack to lowest position and preheat the toaster oven to 425 degrees. Combine 1 tablespoon granulated sugar, lemon juice, cornstarch, and pinch salt in medium bowl. Gently toss peaches with sugar mixture and divide evenly between two 12-ounce ramekins.

2. Combine almonds, flour, brown sugar, cinnamon, nutmeg, remaining pinch salt, and remaining 1 tablespoon granulated sugar in now-empty bowl. Drizzle with melted butter and toss with fork until evenly moistened and mixture

forms large chunks with some pea-size pieces throughout. Sprinkle topping evenly over peaches, breaking up any large chunks.

3. Place ramekins on aluminum foil–lined small rimmed baking sheet and bake until filling is bubbling around edges and topping is deep golden brown, 25 to 30 minutes, rotating sheet halfway through baking. Let crisps cool on wire rack for 15 minutes before serving.

Peach Cobbler

Servings: 4
Cooking Time: 35 Minutes

Ingredients:

- FOR THE FILLING
- 4 cups chopped fresh peaches
- ½ cup sugar
- 2 tablespoons cornstarch
- 1 teaspoon vanilla extract
- FOR THE COBBLER
- 1 cup all-purpose flour
- ¼ cup sugar
- ¾ teaspoon baking powder
- Pinch of sea salt
- 3 tablespoons cold salted butter, cut into ½-inch cubes
- ½ cup buttermilk

Directions:

1. To make the filling
2. In a medium bowl, toss together the peaches, sugar, cornstarch, and vanilla.
3. Transfer to an 8-inch-square baking dish. Set aside.
4. To make the cobbler
5. Place the rack in position 1 and preheat the toaster oven to 350°F on BAKE for 5 minutes.

6. In a large bowl, stir the flour, sugar, baking powder, and sea salt.
7. Using your fingertips, rub the butter into the flour mixture until the mixture resembles coarse crumbs.
8. Add the buttermilk in a thin stream to the flour crumbs, tossing with a fork until a sticky dough forms.
9. Scoop the batter by tablespoons and dollop it on the peaches, spacing the mounds out evenly and leaving gaps for the steam to escape.
10. Bake for 35 minutes, or until the cobbler is golden brown and the filling is bubbly.
11. Serve warm.

Pear Praline Pie

Servings: 10
Cooking Time: 40 Minutes

Ingredients:

- Pie filling:
- 5 pears, peeled, cored, and sliced, or 3 cups sliced canned pears, well drained
- ½ cup dark brown sugar
- ¼ cup unbleached flour
- ½ teaspoon ground ginger
- 1 teaspoon lemon juice
- Salt to taste
- 1 Apple Juice Piecrust, baked
- Praline topping:
- ½ cup brown sugar
- ½ cup chopped pecans
- ½ cup unbleached flour
- 2 tablespoons margarine

Directions:

1. Preheat the toaster oven to 400° F.

2. Combine the pie filling ingredients in a large bowl, mixing well. Spoon the filling into the piecrust shell.

3. Combine the praline topping ingredients in a small bowl, mixing with a fork until crumbly. Sprinkle evenly on top of the pear mixture.

4. BAKE for 40 minutes, or until the pears are tender and the topping is browned.

Pineapple Tartlets

Servings: 4
Cooking Time: 20 Minutes

Ingredients:
- Vegetable oil
- 6 sheets phyllo pastry
- 1 8-ounce can crushed pineapple, drained
- 3 tablespoons low-fat cottage cheese
- 2 tablespoons orange or pineapple marmalade
- 6 teaspoons concentrated thawed frozen orange juice
- Vanilla frozen yogurt or nonfat whipped topping

Directions:
1. Preheat the toaster oven to 350° F.
2. Brush the pans of a 6-muffin tin with vegetable oil. Lay a phyllo sheet on a clean, flat surface and brush with oil. Fold the sheet into quarters to fit the muffin pan. Repeat the process for the remaining phyllo sheets and pans.
3. BAKE for 5 minutes, or until lightly browned. Remove from the oven and cool.
4. Combine the pineapple, cottage cheese, and marmalade in a small bowl, mixing well. Fill the phyllo shells (in the pans) with equal portions of the mixture. Drizzle 1 teaspoon orange juice concentrate over each.
5. BAKE at 400° F. for 15 minutes, or until the filling is cooked. Cool and remove the tartlets carefully from the muffin pans to dessert dishes.

Top with vanilla frozen yogurt or nonfat whipped topping.

Raspberry Hand Pies

Servings: 6
Cooking Time: 20 Minutes

Ingredients:
- 2 cups fresh raspberries
- ¼ cup granulated sugar, plus extra for topping
- 1 tablespoon cornstarch
- 1 tablespoon freshly squeezed lemon juice
- 2 store-bought unbaked pie crusts
- 1 large egg
- 1 tablespoon water
- Oil spray (hand-pumped)

Directions:
1. Preheat the toaster oven to 350°F on AIR FRY for 5 minutes.
2. Place the air-fryer basket in the baking tray.
3. In a medium bowl, stir the raspberries, sugar, cornstarch, and lemon juice until well mixed.
4. Lay the pie crusts on a clean work surface and cut out 6 (6-inch) circles.
5. Evenly divide the raspberry mixture among the circles, placing it in the center.
6. In a small bowl, beat together the egg and water with a fork. Use the egg wash to lightly moisten the edges of the circles, then fold them over to create a half-moon shape. Use a fork to crimp around the rounded part of the pies to seal.
7. Lightly spray the pies with the oil and sprinkle with sugar. Cut 2 to 3 small slits in each pie and place three pies in the basket.
8. In position 2, air fry for 10 minutes until golden brown. Repeat with the remaining pies.
9. Cool the pies and serve.

Apple Strudel

Servings: 2
Cooking Time: 90 Minutes

Ingredients:

- 2 Golden Delicious apples (14 ounces), peeled, cored, and cut into ½-inch pieces
- 1½ tablespoons granulated sugar
- ¼ teaspoon grated lemon zest plus 1 teaspoon juice
- ⅛ teaspoon ground cinnamon
- ⅛ teaspoon ground ginger
- ⅛ teaspoon table salt, divided
- 2 tablespoons golden raisins
- 1 tablespoon panko bread crumbs
- 3½ tablespoons unsalted butter, melted
- 1½ teaspoons confectioners' sugar, plus extra for serving
- 7 (14 by 9-inch) phyllo sheets, thawed

Directions:

1. Toss apples, granulated sugar, lemon zest and juice, cinnamon, ginger, and pinch salt together in large bowl. Cover and microwave until apples are softened, 2 to 4 minutes, stirring once halfway through microwaving. Let apples sit, covered, for 5 minutes. Transfer apples to colander set in second large bowl and let drain, reserving liquid. Return apples to bowl; stir in raisins and panko.

2. Adjust toaster oven rack to middle position and preheat the toaster oven to 350 degrees. Spray small rimmed baking sheet with vegetable oil spray. Stir remaining pinch salt into melted butter.

3. Place 16½ by 12-inch sheet of parchment paper on counter with long side parallel to edge of counter. Place 1 phyllo sheet on parchment with long side parallel to edge of counter. Place confectioners' sugar in fine-mesh strainer. Lightly brush sheet with melted butter and dust sparingly with confectioners' sugar. Repeat with remaining 6 phyllo sheets, melted butter, and confectioners' sugar, stacking sheets one on top of other as you go.

4. Arrange apple mixture in 2½ by 10-inch rectangle 2 inches from bottom of phyllo and about 2 inches from each side. Using parchment fold sides of phyllo over filling, then fold bottom edge of phyllo over filling. Brush folded portions of phyllo with reserved apple liquid. Fold top edge over filling, making sure top and bottom edges overlap by about 1 inch. (If they do not overlap, unfold, rearrange filling into slightly narrower strip, and refold.) Press firmly to seal. Using thin metal spatula, transfer strudel to prepared sheet. Lightly brush top and sides of strudel with remaining apple liquid.

5. Bake until golden brown, 25 to 30 minutes, rotating sheet halfway through baking. Using thin metal spatula, immediately transfer strudel to cutting board. Let cool for 3 minutes. Slice strudel and let cool for at least 20 minutes. Serve warm or at room temperature, dusting with extra confectioners' sugar before serving.

Mixed Berry Hand Pies

Servings: 4
Cooking Time: 15 Minutes

Ingredients:

- ¾ cup sugar
- ½ teaspoon ground cinnamon
- 1 tablespoon cornstarch
- 1 cup blueberries
- 1 cup blackberries
- 1 cup raspberries, divided
- 1 teaspoon water

- 1 package refrigerated pie dough (or your own homemade pie dough)
- 1 egg, beaten

Directions:

1. Combine the sugar, cinnamon, and cornstarch in a small saucepan. Add the blueberries, blackberries, and ½ cup of the raspberries. Toss the berries gently to coat them evenly. Add the teaspoon of water to the saucepan and turn the stovetop on to medium-high heat, stirring occasionally. Once the berries break down, release their juice and start to simmer (about 5 minutes), simmer for another couple of minutes and then transfer the mixture to a bowl, stir in the remaining ½ cup of raspberries and let it cool.

2. Preheat the toaster oven to 370°F.

3. Cut the pie dough into four 5-inch circles and four 6-inch circles.

4. Spread the 6-inch circles on a flat surface. Divide the berry filling between all four circles. Brush the perimeter of the dough circles with a little water. Place the 5-inch circles on top of the filling and press the perimeter of the dough circles together to seal. Roll the edges of the bottom circle up over the top circle to make a crust around the filling. Press a fork around the crust to make decorative indentations and to seal the crust shut. Brush the pies with egg wash and sprinkle a little sugar on top. Poke a small hole in the center of each pie with a paring knife to vent the dough.

5. Air-fry two pies at a time. Brush or spray the air fryer oven with oil and place the pies into the air fryer oven. Air-fry for 9 minutes. Turn the pies over and air-fry for another 6 minutes. Serve warm or at room temperature.

Blueberry Crisp

Servings: 6
Cooking Time: 13 Minutes

Ingredients:

- 3 cups Fresh or thawed frozen blueberries
- ⅓ cup Granulated white sugar
- 1 tablespoon Instant tapioca
- ⅓ cup All-purpose flour
- ⅓ cup Rolled oats (not quick-cooking or steel-cut)
- ⅓ cup Chopped walnuts or pecans
- ⅓ cup Packed light brown sugar
- 5 tablespoons plus 1 teaspoon (⅔ stick) Butter, melted and cooled
- ¾ teaspoon Ground cinnamon
- ¼ teaspoon Table salt

Directions:

1. Preheat the toaster oven to 400°F.

2. Mix the blueberries, granulated white sugar, and instant tapioca in a 6-inch round cake pan for a small batch, a 7-inch round cake pan for a medium batch, or an 8-inch round cake pan for a large batch.

3. When the machine is at temperature, set the cake pan in the air fryer oven and air-fry undisturbed for 5 minutes, or just until the blueberries begin to bubble.

4. Meanwhile, mix the flour, oats, nuts, brown sugar, butter, cinnamon, and salt in a medium bowl until well combined.

5. When the blueberries have begun to bubble, crumble this flour mixture evenly on top. Continue air-frying undisturbed for 8 minutes, or until the topping has browned a bit and the filling is bubbling.

6. Use two hot pads or silicone baking mitts to transfer the cake pan to a wire rack. Cool for at least 10 minutes or to room temperature before serving.

Campfire Banana Boats

Servings: 4
Cooking Time: 20 Minutes

Ingredients:

- 4 medium, unpeeled ripe bananas
- ¼ cup dark chocolate chips
- 4 teaspoons shredded, unsweetened coconut
- ½ cup mini marshmallows
- 4 graham crackers, chopped

Directions:

1. Preheat the toaster oven to 400°F on BAKE for 5 minutes.
2. Cut the bananas lengthwise through the skin about halfway through. Open the pocket to create a space for the other ingredients.
3. Evenly divide the chocolate, coconut, marshmallows, and graham crackers among the bananas.
4. Tear off four 12-inch squares of foil and place the bananas in the center of each. Crimp the foil around the banana to form a boat.
5. Place the bananas on the baking tray, two at a time, and in position 2, bake for 10 minutes until the fillings are gooey and the banana is warmed through.
6. Repeat with the remaining two bananas and serve.

Mississippi Mud Brownies

Servings: 16
Cooking Time: 34 Minutes

Ingredients:

- Nonstick cooking spray
- 3 tablespoons unsweetened cocoa powder
- ¼ cup canola or vegetable oil
- ¼ cup unsalted butter, softened
- 1 cup granulated sugar
- 2 large eggs
- 1 teaspoon pure vanilla extract
- ¾ cup all-purpose flour
- ½ teaspoon table salt
- ½ cup pecan pieces, toasted
- 2 cups mini marshmallows
- FROSTING
- ¼ cup unsalted butter, melted
- 3 tablespoons unsweetened cocoa powder
- ½ teaspoon pure vanilla extract
- 2 cups confectioners' sugar
- 2 to 3 tablespoons whole milk

Directions:

1. Preheat the toaster oven to 350°F. Spray an 8-inch square baking pan with nonstick cooking spray.
2. Beat the cocoa and oil in a large bowl with a handheld mixer at medium speed. Add the butter and mix until smooth. Beat in the granulated sugar. Add the eggs, one at a time, mixing after each addition. Add the vanilla and mix. On low speed, blend in the flour and salt. Stir in the pecans.
3. Pour the batter into the prepared pan. Bake for 28 to 32 minutes, or until a wooden pick inserted into the center comes out clean.
4. Remove the brownies from the oven and sprinkle the marshmallows over the top. Return to the oven and bake for about 2 minutes or until the marshmallows are puffed. Place on a wire rack and let cool completely.
5. Meanwhile, make the frosting: Combine the butter, cocoa, vanilla, confectioners' sugar, and 2 tablespoons milk in a large bowl. Beat until smooth. If needed for the desired consistency, add additional milk. Frost the cooled brownies.

Dark Chocolate Banana Bread

Servings: 8

Cooking Time: 60 Minutes

Ingredients:

- ½ cup salted butter, melted, plus extra for greasing the pan
- 1 cup all-purpose flour, plus extra for dusting the pan
- ¾ cup dark brown sugar
- ¼ cup cocoa powder
- 2 teaspoons baking powder
- ¼ teaspoon sea salt
- 2 large bananas, mashed
- 1 large egg
- 1½ teaspoons vanilla extract
- ½ cup dark chocolate chips

Directions:

1. Place the rack in position 1 and preheat the oven to 325°F on BAKE for 5 minutes.

2. Grease a 9-by-5-inch loaf pan with melted butter and dust with all-purpose flour. Set aside.

3. In a medium bowl, stir the flour, brown sugar, cocoa powder, baking powder, and salt together until well combined.

4. In a medium bowl, whisk the butter, bananas, egg, and vanilla until well blended.

5. Add the wet ingredients to the dry ingredients and stir until combined. Add the chocolate chips and stir until incorporated.

6. Bake for 1 hour, or until a toothpick inserted into the center of the bread comes out mostly clean. If the bread starts to get too dark, cover the top with foil and bake until done.

7. Let the bread cool for 10 minutes and then run a knife around the edge and remove the bread from the loaf pan to cool completely on a rack.

8. Serve when cool.

POULTRY

Quick Chicken For Filling

Servings: 2
Cooking Time: 8 Minutes

Ingredients:

- 1 pound chicken tenders, skinless and boneless
- ½ teaspoon ground cumin
- ½ teaspoon garlic powder
- cooking spray

Directions:

1. Sprinkle raw chicken tenders with seasonings.
2. Spray air fryer oven lightly with cooking spray to prevent sticking.
3. Place chicken in air fryer oven in single layer.
4. Air-fry at 390°F for 4 minutes, turn chicken strips over, and air-fry for an additional 4 minutes.
5. Test for doneness. Thick tenders may require an additional minute or two.

Tasty Meat Loaf

Servings: 4
Cooking Time: 35 Minutes

Ingredients:

- 1 to 1½ pounds ground turkey or chicken breast
- 1 egg
- 1 tablespoon chopped fresh parsley
- 2 tablespoons chopped bell pepper
- 3 tablespoons chopped canned mushrooms
- 2 tablespoons chopped onion
- 2 garlic cloves, minced
- ½ cup multigrain bread crumbs
- 1 tablespoon Worcestershire sauce
- 1 tablespoon ketchup
- Freshly ground black pepper to taste

Directions:

1. Preheat the toaster oven to 400° F.
2. Combine all the ingredients in a large bowl and press into a regular-size 4½ × 8½ × 2¼-inch loaf pan.
3. BAKE for 35 minutes, or until browned on top.

Crispy Curry Chicken Tenders

Servings: 4
Cooking Time: 14 Minutes

Ingredients:

- 1 pound boneless skinless chicken tenders
- ¼ cup plain yogurt
- 2 tablespoons thai red curry paste
- 1½ teaspoons salt, divided
- ½ teaspoon pepper
- 1¾ cups panko breadcrumbs
- 1 teaspoon granulated garlic
- 1 teaspoon granulated onion
- Olive oil or avocado oil spray

Directions:

1. Whisk together the yogurt, curry paste, 1 teaspoon of salt, and pepper in a large bowl. Add the chicken tenders and toss to coat. Cover bowl with plastic wrap and marinate in the fridge for 6-8 hours.
2. Combine the panko breadcrumbs, ½ teaspoon salt, garlic, and onion. Remove chicken tenders from the marinade and coat individually in the panko mixture.
3. Preheat the toaster oven to 430°F.

4. Spray both sides of each chicken tender well with olive oil or avocado oil spray, then place into the fry basket.

5. Insert the fry basket at mid position in the preheated oven.

6. Select the Air Fry and Shake functions, adjust time to 14 minutes, and press Start/Pause.

7. Flip chicken tenders halfway through cooking. The Shake Reminder will let you know when.

8. Remove when chicken tenders are golden and crispy.

Tandoori Chicken Legs

Servings: 2
Cooking Time: 30 Minutes

Ingredients:

- 1 cup plain yogurt
- 2 cloves garlic, minced
- 1 tablespoon grated fresh ginger
- 2 teaspoons paprika
- 2 teaspoons ground coriander
- 1 teaspoon ground turmeric
- 1 teaspoon salt
- ¼ teaspoon ground cayenne pepper
- juice of 1 lime
- 2 bone-in, skin-on chicken legs
- fresh cilantro leaves

Directions:

1. Make the marinade by combining the yogurt, garlic, ginger, spices and lime juice. Make slashes into the chicken legs to help the marinade penetrate the meat. Pour the marinade over the chicken legs, cover and let the chicken marinate for at least an hour or overnight in the refrigerator.

2. Preheat the toaster oven oven to 380°F.

3. Transfer the chicken legs from the marinade to the air fryer oven, reserving any extra marinade.

Air-fry for 15 minutes. Flip the chicken over and pour the remaining marinade over the top. Air-fry for another 15 minutes, watching to make sure it doesn't brown too much. If it does start to get too brown, you can loosely tent the chicken with aluminum foil, tucking the ends of the foil under the chicken to stop it from blowing around.

4. Serve over rice with some fresh cilantro on top.

Sesame Orange Chicken

Servings: 2
Cooking Time: 9 Minutes

Ingredients:

- 1 pound boneless, skinless chicken breasts, cut into cubes
- salt and freshly ground black pepper
- ¼ cup cornstarch
- 2 eggs, beaten
- 1½ cups panko breadcrumbs
- vegetable or peanut oil, in a spray bottle
- 12 ounces orange marmalade
- 1 tablespoon soy sauce
- 1 teaspoon minced ginger
- 2 tablespoons hoisin sauce
- 1 tablespoon sesame oil
- sesame seeds, toasted

Directions:

1. Season the chicken pieces with salt and pepper. Set up a dredging station. Put the cornstarch in a zipper-sealable plastic bag. Place the beaten eggs in a bowl and put the panko breadcrumbs in a shallow dish. Transfer the seasoned chicken to the bag with the cornstarch and shake well to completely coat the chicken on all sides. Remove the chicken from the bag, shaking off any excess cornstarch and dip the

pieces into the egg. Let any excess egg drip from the chicken and transfer into the breadcrumbs, pressing the crumbs onto the chicken pieces with your hands. Spray the chicken pieces with vegetable or peanut oil.

2. Preheat the toaster oven to 400°F.

3. Combine the orange marmalade, soy sauce, ginger, hoisin sauce and sesame oil in a saucepan. Bring the mixture to a boil on the stovetop, lower the heat and simmer for 10 minutes, until the sauce has thickened. Set aside and keep warm.

4. Transfer the coated chicken to the air fryer oven and air-fry at 400°F for 9 minutes, rotate a few times during the cooking process to help the chicken cook evenly.

5. Right before serving, toss the browned chicken pieces with the sesame orange sauce. Serve over white rice with steamed broccoli. Sprinkle the sesame seeds on top.

Chicken Pot Pie

Servings: 4
Cooking Time: 65 Minutes

Ingredients:
- ¼ cup salted butter
- 1 small sweet onion, chopped
- 1 carrot, chopped
- 1 teaspoon minced garlic
- ¼ cup all-purpose flour
- 1 cup low-sodium chicken broth
- ¼ cup heavy (whipping) cream
- 2 cups diced store-bought rotisserie chicken
- 1 cup frozen peas
- Sea salt, for seasoning
- Freshly ground black pepper, for seasoning
- 1 unbaked store-bought pie crust

Directions:

1. Place the rack in position 1 and preheat the toaster oven to 350°F on BAKE for 5 minutes.

2. Melt the butter in a large saucepan over medium-high heat. Sauté the onion, carrot, and garlic until softened, about 12 minutes. Whisk in the flour to form a thick paste and whisk for 1 minute to cook.

3. Add the broth and whisk until thickened, about 2 minutes. Add the heavy cream, whisking to combine. Add the chicken and peas, and season with salt and pepper.

4. Transfer the filling to a 1½-quart casserole dish and top with the pie crust, tucking the edges into the sides of the casserole dish to completely enclose the filling. Cut 4 or 5 slits in the top of the crust.

5. Bake for 50 minutes until the crust is golden brown and the filling is bubbly. Serve.

Chicken Potpie

Servings: 4
Cooking Time: 48 Minutes

Ingredients:
- Pie filling:
- 1 tablespoon unbleached flour
- ½ cup evaporated skim milk
- 4 skinless, boneless chicken thighs, cut into 1-inch cubes
- 1 cup potatoes, peeled and cut into ½-inch pieces
- ½ cup frozen green peas
- ½ cup thinly sliced carrot
- 2 tablespoons chopped onion
- ½ cup chopped celery
- 1 teaspoon garlic powder
- Salt and freshly ground black pepper to taste
- 8 sheets phyllo pastry, thawed Olive oil

Directions:

1. Preheat the toaster oven to 400° F.

2. Whisk the flour into the milk until smooth in a 1-quart 8½ × 8½ × 4-inch ovenproof baking dish. Add the remaining filling ingredients and mix well. Adjust the seasonings to taste. Cover the dish with aluminum foil.

3. BAKE for 40 minutes, or until the carrot, potatoes, and celery are tender. Remove from the oven and uncover.

4. Place one sheet of phyllo pastry on top of the baked pie-filling mixture, bending the edges to fit the shape of the baking dish. Brush the sheet with olive oil. Add another sheet on top of it and brush with oil. Continue adding the remaining sheets, brushing each one, until the crust is completed. Brush the top with oil.

5. BAKE for 6 minutes, or until the phyllo pastry is browned.

Roast Chicken

Servings: 6
Cooking Time: 90 Minutes

Ingredients:
- Nonstick cooking spray
- 1 whole (3 ½ -pound) chicken
- Grated zest and juice of 1 lemon
- 1 tablespoon olive oil
- 1 ½ teaspoons kosher salt
- 1 teaspoon garlic powder
- ½ teaspoon dried thyme leaves
- ½ teaspoon freshly ground black pepper

Directions:

1. Preheat the toaster oven to 350°F. Spray a 12 x 12-inch baking pan with nonstick cooking spray.

2. Drizzle the chicken cavity with about half of the lemon juice. Place half of the juiced lemon into the chicken cavity. Truss the chicken using kitchen twine.

3. Rub the chicken evenly with the olive oil.

4. Stir the salt, garlic powder, lemon zest, thyme, and pepper in a small bowl. Using your fingertips, rub the seasonings evenly over the chicken. Place the chicken, breast side up, in the prepared pan. Drizzle with the remaining lemon juice.

5. Roast, uncovered, for 1 ¼ hours to 1 ½ hours, or until a meat thermometer registers 165°F. Let stand for 10 minutes before carving.

Mediterranean Stuffed Chicken Breasts

Servings: 4
Cooking Time: 24 Minutes

Ingredients:
- 4 boneless, skinless chicken breasts
- ½ teaspoon salt
- ½ teaspoon black pepper
- ½ teaspoon garlic powder
- ½ teaspoon paprika
- ½ cup canned artichoke hearts, chopped
- 4 ounces cream cheese
- ¼ cup grated Parmesan cheese

Directions:

1. Pat the chicken breasts with a paper towel. Using a sharp knife, cut a pouch in the side of each chicken breast for filling.

2. In a small bowl, mix the salt, pepper, garlic powder, and paprika. Season the chicken breasts with this mixture.

3. In a medium bowl, mix together the artichokes, cream cheese, and grated Parmesan cheese. Divide the filling between the 4 breasts, stuffing it inside the pouches. Use toothpicks to close the pouches and secure the filling.

4. Preheat the toaster oven to 360°F.

5. Spray the air fryer oven liberally with cooking spray, add the stuffed chicken breasts to the air fryer oven, and spray liberally with cooking spray again. Air-fry for 14 minutes, carefully turn over the chicken breasts, and cook another 10 minutes. Check the temperature at 20 minutes cooking. Chicken breasts are fully cooked when the center measures 165°F. Cook in batches, if needed.

Chicken Parmesan

Servings: 4
Cooking Time: 11 Minutes

Ingredients:
- 4 chicken tenders
- Italian seasoning
- salt
- ¼ cup cornstarch
- ½ cup Italian salad dressing
- ¼ cup panko breadcrumbs
- ¼ cup grated Parmesan cheese, plus more for serving
- oil for misting or cooking spray
- 8 ounces spaghetti, cooked
- 1 24-ounce jar marinara sauce

Directions:
1. Pound chicken tenders with meat mallet or rolling pin until about ¼-inch thick.
2. Sprinkle both sides with Italian seasoning and salt to taste.
3. Place cornstarch and salad dressing in 2 separate shallow dishes.
4. In a third shallow dish, mix together the panko crumbs and Parmesan cheese.
5. Dip flattened chicken in cornstarch, then salad dressing. Dip in the panko mixture, pressing into the chicken so the coating sticks well.

6. Spray both sides with oil or cooking spray Place in air fryer oven in single layer.

7. Air-fry at 390°F for 5 minutes. Spray with oi again, turning chicken to coat both sides. See tip about turning.

8. Air-fry for an additional 6 minutes or unti chicken juices run clear and outside is browned.

9. While chicken is cooking, heat marinara sauce and stir into cooked spaghetti.

10. To serve, divide spaghetti with sauce among 4 dinner plates, and top each with a fried chicker tender. Pass additional Parmesan at the table for those who want extra cheese.

Chicken Souvlaki Gyros

Servings: 4
Cooking Time: 18 Minutes

Ingredients:
- ¼ cup extra-virgin olive oil
- 1 clove garlic, crushed
- 1 tablespoon Italian seasoning
- ½ teaspoon paprika
- ½ lemon, sliced
- ¼ teaspoon salt
- 1 pound boneless, skinless chicken breasts
- 4 whole-grain pita breads
- 1 cup shredded lettuce
- ½ cup chopped tomatoes
- ¼ cup chopped red onion
- ¼ cup cucumber yogurt sauce

Directions:
1. In a large resealable plastic bag, combine the olive oil, garlic, Italian seasoning, paprika, lemon, and salt. Add the chicken to the bag and secure shut. Vigorously shake until all the ingredients are combined. Set in the fridge for 2 hours to marinate.

2. When ready to cook, preheat the toaster oven to 360°F.

3. Liberally spray the air fryer oven with olive oil mist. Remove the chicken from the bag and discard the leftover marinade. Place the chicken into the air fryer oven, allowing enough room between the chicken breasts to flip.

4. Air-fry for 10 minutes, flip, and cook another 8 minutes.

5. Remove the chicken from the air fryer oven when it has cooked (or the internal temperature of the chicken reaches 165°F). Let rest 5 minutes. Then thinly slice the chicken into strips.

6. Assemble the gyros by placing the pita bread on a flat surface and topping with chicken, lettuce, tomatoes, onion, and a drizzle of yogurt sauce.

7. Serve warm.

Peanut Butter-barbeque Chicken

Servings: 4

Cooking Time: 20 Minutes

Ingredients:

- 1 pound boneless, skinless chicken thighs
- salt and pepper
- 1 large orange
- ½ cup barbeque sauce
- 2 tablespoons smooth peanut butter
- 2 tablespoons chopped peanuts for garnish (optional)
- cooking spray

Directions:

1. Season chicken with salt and pepper to taste. Place in a shallow dish or plastic bag.

2. Grate orange peel, squeeze orange and reserve 1 tablespoon of juice for the sauce.

3. Pour remaining juice over chicken and marinate for 30 minutes.

4. Mix together the reserved 1 tablespoon of orange juice, barbeque sauce, peanut butter, and 1 teaspoon grated orange peel.

5. Place ¼ cup of sauce mixture in a small bowl for basting. Set remaining sauce aside to serve with cooked chicken.

6. Preheat the toaster oven to 360°F. Spray air fryer oven with nonstick cooking spray.

7. Remove chicken from marinade, letting excess drip off. Place in air fryer oven and air-fry for 5 minutes. Turn chicken over and cook 5 minutes longer.

8. Brush both sides of chicken lightly with sauce.

9. Cook chicken 5 minutes, then turn thighs one more time, again brushing both sides lightly with sauce. Air-fry for 5 more minutes or until chicken is done and juices run clear.

10. Serve chicken with remaining sauce on the side and garnish with chopped peanuts if you like.

Fried Chicken

Servings: 4

Cooking Time: 40 Minutes

Ingredients:

- 12 skin-on chicken drumsticks
- 1 cup buttermilk
- 1½ cups all-purpose flour
- 1 tablespoon smoked paprika
- ¾ teaspoon celery salt
- ¾ teaspoon dried mustard
- ½ teaspoon garlic powder
- ½ teaspoon freshly ground black pepper
- ½ teaspoon sea salt
- ½ teaspoon dried thyme
- ¼ teaspoon dried oregano
- 4 large eggs
- Oil spray (hand-pumped)

Directions:

1. Place the chicken and buttermilk in a medium bowl, cover, and refrigerate for at least 1 hour, up to overnight.

2. Preheat the toaster oven to 375°F on AIR FRY for 5 minutes.

3. In a large bowl, stir the flour, paprika, celery salt, mustard, garlic powder, pepper, salt, thyme, and oregano until well mixed.

4. Beat the eggs until frothy in a medium bowl and set them beside the flour.

5. Place the air-fryer basket in the baking tray and generously spray it with the oil.

6. Dredge a chicken drumstick in the flour, then the eggs, and then in the flour again, thickly coating it, and place the drumstick in the basket. Repeat with 5 more drumsticks and spray them all lightly with the oil on all sides.

7. In position 2, air fry for 20 minutes, turning halfway through, until golden brown and crispy with an internal temperature of 165°F.

8. Repeat with the remaining chicken, covering the cooked chicken loosely with foil to keep it warm. Serve.

Buffalo Egg Rolls

Servings: 8
Cooking Time: 9 Minutes

Ingredients:

- 1 teaspoon water
- 1 tablespoon cornstarch
- 1 egg
- 2½ cups cooked chicken, diced or shredded (see opposite page)
- ⅓ cup chopped green onion
- ⅓ cup diced celery
- ⅓ cup buffalo wing sauce
- 8 egg roll wraps
- oil for misting or cooking spray
- Blue Cheese Dip
- 3 ounces cream cheese, softened
- ⅓ cup blue cheese, crumbled
- 1 teaspoon Worcestershire sauce
- ¼ teaspoon garlic powder
- ¼ cup buttermilk (or sour cream)

Directions:

1. Mix water and cornstarch in a small bowl until dissolved. Add egg, beat well, and set aside.

2. In a medium size bowl, mix together chicken, green onion, celery, and buffalo wing sauce.

3. Divide chicken mixture evenly among 8 egg roll wraps, spooning ½ inch from one edge.

4. Moisten all edges of each wrap with beaten egg wash.

5. Fold the short ends over filling, then roll up tightly and press to seal edges.

6. Brush outside of wraps with egg wash, then spritz with oil or cooking spray.

7. Place 4 egg rolls in air fryer oven.

8. Air-fry at 390°F for 9 minutes or until outside is brown and crispy.

9. While the rolls are cooking, prepare the Blue Cheese Dip. With a fork, mash together cream cheese and blue cheese.

10. Stir in remaining ingredients.

11. Dip should be just thick enough to slightly cling to egg rolls. If too thick, stir in buttermilk or milk 1 tablespoon at a time until you reach the desired consistency.

12. Cook remaining 4 egg rolls as in steps 7 and 8.

13. Serve while hot with Blue Cheese Dip, more buffalo wing sauce, or both.

Crispy "fried" Chicken

Servings: 4

Cooking Time: 14 Minutes

Ingredients:

- ¾ cup all-purpose flour
- ½ teaspoon paprika
- ¼ teaspoon black pepper
- ¼ teaspoon salt
- 2 large eggs
- 1½ cups panko breadcrumbs
- 1 pound boneless, skinless chicken tenders

Directions:

1. Preheat the toaster oven to 400°F.
2. In a shallow bowl, mix the flour with the paprika, pepper, and salt.
3. In a separate bowl, whisk the eggs; set aside.
4. In a third bowl, place the breadcrumbs.
5. Liberally spray the air fryer oven with olive oil spray.
6. Pat the chicken tenders dry with a paper towel. Dredge the tenders one at a time in the flour, then dip them in the egg, and toss them in the breadcrumb coating. Repeat until all tenders are coated.
7. Set each tender in the air fryer oven, leaving room on each side of the tender to allow for flipping.
8. When the air fryer oven is full, cook 4 to 7 minutes, flip, and cook another 4 to 7 minutes.
9. Remove the tenders and let cool 5 minutes before serving. Repeat until all tenders are cooked.

Coconut Chicken With Apricot-ginger Sauce

Servings: 4

Cooking Time: 8 Minutes

Ingredients:

- 1½ pounds boneless, skinless chicken tenders, cut in large chunks (about 1¼ inches)
- salt and pepper
- ½ cup cornstarch
- 2 eggs
- 1 tablespoon milk
- 3 cups shredded coconut (see below)
- oil for misting or cooking spray
- Apricot-Ginger Sauce
- ½ cup apricot preserves
- 2 tablespoons white vinegar
- ¼ teaspoon ground ginger
- ¼ teaspoon low-sodium soy sauce
- 2 teaspoons white or yellow onion, grated or finely minced

Directions:

1. Mix all ingredients for the Apricot-Ginger Sauce well and let sit for flavors to blend while you cook the chicken.
2. Season chicken chunks with salt and pepper to taste.
3. Place cornstarch in a shallow dish.
4. In another shallow dish, beat together eggs and milk.
5. Place coconut in a third shallow dish. (If also using panko breadcrumbs, as suggested below, stir them to mix well.)
6. Spray air fryer oven with oil or cooking spray.
7. Dip each chicken chunk into cornstarch, shake off excess, and dip in egg mixture.
8. Shake off excess egg mixture and roll lightly in coconut or coconut mixture. Spray with oil.
9. Place coated chicken chunks in air fryer oven in a single layer, close together but without sides touching.

10. Air-fry at 360°F for 4 minutes, stop, and turn chunks over.

11. Cook an additional 4 minutes or until chicken is done inside and coating is crispy brown.

12. Repeat steps 9 through 11 to cook remaining chicken chunks.

Harissa Lemon Whole Chicken

Servings: 6
Cooking Time: 60 Minutes

Ingredients:

- 2 teaspoons kosher salt
- ½ teaspoon freshly ground black pepper
- ½ teaspoon ground cumin
- 2 garlic cloves
- 6 tablespoons harissa paste
- ½ lemon, juiced
- 1 whole lemon, zested
- 1 (5 pound) whole chicken

Directions:

1. Place salt, pepper, cumin, garlic cloves, harissa paste, lemon juice, and lemon zest in a food processor and pulse until they form a smooth puree.

2. Rub the puree all over the chicken, especially inside the cavity, and cover with plastic wrap.

3. Marinate for 1 hour at room temperature.

4. Preheat the toaster oven to 350°F.

5. Place the marinated chicken on the food tray, then insert the tray at low position in the preheated oven.

6. Select the Roast function, then press Start/Pause.

7. Remove when done, tent chicken with foil, and allow it to rest for 20 minutes before serving.

I Forgot To Thaw—garlic Capered Chicken Thighs

Servings: 4
Cooking Time: 50 Minutes

Ingredients:

- 6 frozen skinless, boneless chicken thighs
- Garlic mixture:
- 3 garlic cloves, minced
- ¾ cup dry white wine
- 2 tablespoons capers
- ½ teaspoon paprika
- ¼ teaspoon ground cumin
- Salt and freshly ground black pepper to taste

Directions:

1. Preheat the toaster oven to 400° F.

2. Thaw the chicken as directed. Separate the pieces and add the garlic mixture, which has been combined in a small bowl, stirring well to coat. Cover the dish with aluminum foil.

3. BAKE for 30 minutes, or until the chicken is tender. Remove the cover and turn the chicken pieces, spooning the sauce over them.

4. BROIL for 8 minutes, or until the chicken is lightly browned.

Spice-rubbed Split Game Hen

Servings: 2
Cooking Time: 48 Minutes

Ingredients:

- Spice rub mixture:
- 1 teaspoon ground cumin
- 1 teaspoon garlic powder
- 1 teaspoon onion powder
- 1 teaspoon paprika
- 1 teaspoon ground coriander
- 1 teaspoon salt (optional)

- 1 Cornish game hen, split

Directions:

1. Preheat the toaster oven to 400° F.

2. Mix all the spices together in a small bowl and rub each half of the game hen well and on both sides to coat evenly. Place the pieces skin side down in a baking dish. Cover the dish with aluminum foil.

3. BAKE for 20 minutes. Turn the pieces over and bake, covered, for another 20 minutes, or until the meat is tender. Remove from the oven and uncover.

4. BROIL 8 minutes, or until browned to your preference.

Marinated Green Pepper And Pineapple Chicken

Servings: 4
Cooking Time: 20 Minutes

Ingredients:

- Marinade:
- 1 teaspoon finely chopped fresh ginger
- 2 garlic cloves, finely chopped
- 1 teaspoon toasted sesame oil
- 1 tablespoon brown sugar
- 2 tablespoons soy sauce
- ¾ cup dry white wine
- 2 skinless, boneless chicken breasts, cut into 1 × 3-inch strips
- 2 tablespoons chopped onion
- 1 bell pepper, chopped
- 1 5-ounce can pineapple chunks, drained
- 2 tablespoons grated unsweetened coconut

Directions:

1. Combine the marinade ingredients in a medium bowl and blend well. Add the chicken

strips and spoon the mixture over them. Marinate in the refrigerator for at least 1 hour. Remove the strips from the marinade and place in an oiled or nonstick 8½ × 8½ × 2-inch square (cake) pan. Add the onion and pepper and mix well.

2. BROIL for 8 minutes. Then remove from the oven and, using tongs, turn the chicken, pepper, and onion pieces. (Spoon the reserved marinade over the pieces, if desired.)

3. BROIL again for 8 minutes, or until the chicken, pepper, and onion are cooked through and tender. Add the pineapple chunks and coconut and toss to mix well.

4. BROIL for another 4 minutes, or until the coconut is lightly browned.

Sweet-and-sour Chicken

Servings: 6
Cooking Time: 10 Minutes

Ingredients:

- 1 cup pineapple juice
- 1 cup plus 3 tablespoons cornstarch, divided
- ¼ cup sugar
- ¼ cup ketchup
- ¼ cup apple cider vinegar
- 2 tablespoons soy sauce or tamari
- 1 teaspoon garlic powder, divided
- ¼ cup flour
- 1 tablespoon sesame seeds
- ½ teaspoon salt
- ¼ teaspoon ground black pepper
- 2 large eggs
- 2 pounds chicken breasts, cut into 1-inch cubes
- 1 red bell pepper, cut into 1-inch pieces
- 1 carrot, sliced into ¼-inch-thick rounds

Directions:

1. In a medium saucepan, whisk together the pineapple juice, 3 tablespoons of the cornstarch, the sugar, the ketchup, the apple cider vinegar, the soy sauce or tamari, and ½ teaspoon of the garlic powder. Cook over medium-low heat, whisking occasionally as the sauce thickens, about 6 minutes. Stir and set aside while preparing the chicken.

2. Preheat the toaster oven to 370°F.

3. In a medium bowl, place the remaining 1 cup of cornstarch, the flour, the sesame seeds, the salt, the remaining ½ teaspoon of garlic powder, and the pepper.

4. In a second medium bowl, whisk the eggs.

5. Working in batches, place the cubed chicken in the cornstarch mixture to lightly coat; then dip it into the egg mixture, and return it to the cornstarch mixture. Shake off the excess and place the coated chicken in the air fryer oven. Spray with cooking spray and air-fry for 5 minutes, and spray with more cooking spray. Cook an additional 3 to 5 minutes, or until completely cooked and golden brown.

6. On the last batch of chicken, add the bell pepper and carrot to the air fryer oven and cook with the chicken.

7. Place the cooked chicken and vegetables into a serving bowl and toss with the sweet-and-sour sauce to serve.

Oven-crisped Chicken

Servings: 4
Cooking Time: 35 Minutes

Ingredients:
- Coating mixture:
- 1 cup cornmeal
- ¼ cup wheat germ
- 1 teaspoon paprika
- 1 teaspoon garlic powder
- Salt and butcher's pepper to taste
- 3 tablespoons olive oil
- 1 tablespoon spicy brown mustard
- 6 skinless, boneless chicken thighs

Directions:
1. Preheat the toaster oven to 375° F.

2. Combine the coating mixture ingredients in a small bowl and transfer to a plate, spreading the mixture evenly over the plate's surface. Set aside.

3. Whisk together the oil and mustard in a bowl. Add the chicken pieces and toss to coat thoroughly. Press both sides of each piece into the coating mixture to coat well. Chill in the refrigerator for 10 minutes. Transfer the chicken pieces to a broiling rack with a pan underneath.

4. BAKE, uncovered, for 35 minutes, or until the meat is tender and the coating is crisp and golden brown or browned to your preference.

Air-fried Turkey Breast With Cherry Glaze

Servings: 6
Cooking Time: 54 Minutes

Ingredients:
- 1 (5-pound) turkey breast
- 2 teaspoons olive oil
- 1 teaspoon dried thyme
- ½ teaspoon dried sage
- 1 teaspoon salt
- ½ teaspoon freshly ground black pepper
- ½ cup cherry preserves
- 1 tablespoon chopped fresh thyme leaves
- 1 teaspoon soy sauce
- freshly ground black pepper

Directions:

1. All turkeys are built differently, so depending on the turkey breast and how your butcher has prepared it, you may need to trim the bottom of the ribs in order to get the turkey to sit upright in the air fryer oven without touching the heating element. The key to this recipe is getting the right size turkey breast. Once you've managed that, the rest is easy, so make sure your turkey breast fits into the air fryer oven before you Preheat the toaster oven oven.

2. Preheat the toaster oven to 350°F.

3. Brush the turkey breast all over with the olive oil. Combine the thyme, sage, salt and pepper and rub the outside of the turkey breast with the spice mixture.

4. Transfer the seasoned turkey breast to the air fryer oven, breast side up, and air-fry at 350°F for 25 minutes. Turn the turkey breast on its side and air-fry for another 12 minutes. Turn the turkey breast on the opposite side and air-fry for 12 more minutes. The internal temperature of the turkey breast should reach 165°F when fully cooked.

5. While the turkey is air-frying, make the glaze by combining the cherry preserves, fresh thyme, soy sauce and pepper in a small bowl. When the cooking time is up, return the turkey breast to an upright position and brush the glaze all over the turkey. Air-fry for a final 5 minutes, until the skin is nicely browned and crispy. Let the turkey rest, loosely tented with foil, for at least 5 minutes before slicing and serving.

Chicken Chunks

Servings: 4
Cooking Time: 10 Minutes

Ingredients:

- 1 pound chicken tenders cut in large chunks, about 1½ inches
- salt and pepper
- ½ cup cornstarch
- 2 eggs, beaten
- 1 cup panko breadcrumbs
- oil for misting or cooking spray

Directions:

1. Season chicken chunks to your liking with salt and pepper.

2. Dip chicken chunks in cornstarch. Then dip in egg and shake off excess. Then roll in panko crumbs to coat well.

3. Spray all sides of chicken chunks with oil or cooking spray.

4. Place chicken in air fryer oven in single layer and air-fry at 390°F for 5 minutes. Spray with oil, turn chunks over, and spray other side.

5. Air-fry for an additional 5 minutes or until chicken juices run clear and outside is golden brown.

6. Repeat steps 4 and 5 to cook remaining chicken.

RECIPE INDEX

Lima Bean And Artichoke Casserole 34
Little Swedish Coffee Cakes 98

M

Mahi Mahi Tacos With Pineapple Salsa 20
Maple Bacon 31
Marinated Green Pepper And Pineapple Chicken 115
Mediterranean Baked Fish 59
Mediterranean Stuffed Chicken Breasts 109
Minted Lamb Chops 67
Miso-glazed Salmon With Broccoli 29
Miso-rubbed Salmon Fillets 57
Mississippi Mud Brownies 104
Mixed Berry Hand Pies 102
Molasses Baked Beans 88
Morning Glory Muffins 25
Mozzarella-stuffed Arancini 39

N

Nacho Chips 20

O

Oat Bran Muffins 21
Oatmeal Piecrust 19
Onion And Cheese Buttermilk Biscuits 25
Orange-glazed Pears 14
Oven-baked Barley 30
Oven-baked Couscous 32
Oven-baked Reuben 21
Oven-crisped Chicken 116
Oysters Broiled In Wine Sauce 63

P

Panzanella Salad With Crispy Croutons 81
Parmesan Asparagus 80
Parmesan Garlic French Fries 50
Parmesan Garlic Fries 84
Parmesan Peas 49
Pea Soup 33

Peach Cobbler 100
Peanut Butter-barbeque Chicken 111
Pear Praline Pie 100
Pecan Parmesan Cauliflower 88
Pecan-crusted Tilapia 62
Pecan-topped Baked Oatmeal 18
Pecan-topped Sole 55
Pesto Pork Chops 75
Pineapple Tartlets 101
Potato Skins 90
Pretzel-coated Pork Tenderloin 68

Q

Quick Broccoli Quiche 87
Quick Chicken For Filling 106

R

Raspberry Hand Pies 101
Red Curry Flank Steak 67
Ribeye Steak With Blue Cheese Compound Butter 74
Roast Chicken 109
Roasted Brussels Sprouts Au Gratin 42
Roasted Cauliflower With Garlic And Capers 88
Roasted Eggplant Halves With Herbed Ricotta 89
Roasted Fennel With Wine + Parmesan 45
Roasted Green Beans With Goat Cheese And Hazelnuts 46
Roasted Vegetable Gazpacho 30
Rolled Asparagus Flounder 58
Rosemary Lentils 36
Rosemary New Potatoes 86

S

Sage, Chicken + Mushroom Pasta Casserole 31
Salad Lentils 34
Salt And Pepper Baked Potatoes 83
Sea Bass With Potato Scales And Caper Aïoli 61

CPSIA information can be obtained
at www.ICGtesting.com
Printed in the USA
BVHW010440260122
627128BV00005B/297